MW00570714

Jim Burns's work represents his integrity, intelligence, and his heart for kids. The *Uncommon* high school group studies will change some lives and save many others.

stephen arterburn
Bestselling Author, *Every Man's Battle*

Jim Burns has found the right balance between learning God's Word and applying it to life. The topics are relevant, up to date and on target. Jim gets kids to think. This is a terrific series, and I highly recommend it.

les j. christie
Chair of Youth Ministry, William Jessup University, Rocklin, California

There are very few people in the world who know how to communicate life-changing truth effectively to teens. Jim Burns is one of the best. These studies are biblically sound, hands-on practical and just plain fun. This one gets a five-star endorsement.

ken davis
Author and Speaker (www.kendavis.com)

I don't know anyone who knows and understands the needs of the youth worker like Jim Burns. The *Uncommon* high school group studies are solid, easy to use and get students out of their seats and into the Word.

doug fields
Senior Director of HomeWord Center for Youth and Family @ Azusa Pacific University
Simply Youth Ministry (www.simplyyouthministry.com)

The practicing youth worker always needs more ammunition. The *Uncommon* high school group studies will get that blank stare off the faces of the kids at your youth meeting!

jay kesler
President Emeritus, Taylor University, Upland, Indiana

In the *Uncommon* high school group studies, Jim Burns pulls together the key ingredients for an effective series. He captures the combination of teen involvement and a solid biblical perspective with topics that are relevant and straightforward. This will be a valuable tool in the local church.

dennis "tiger" mcluen
Executive Director, Youth Leadership (www.youthleadership.com)

Young people need the information necessary to make wise decisions related to everyday problems. The *Uncommon* high school group studies will help many young people integrate their faith into everyday life, which, after all, is our goal as youth workers.

miles mcpherson
Senior Pastor, The Rock Church, San Diego, California

This is a resource that is user-friendly, learner-centered and intentionally biblical. I love having a resource like this that I can recommend to youth ministry volunteers and professionals.

duffy robbins
Professor of Youth Ministry, Eastern University, St. Davids, Pennsylvania

The *Uncommon* high school group studies provide the motivation and information for leaders and the types of experience and content that will capture high school people. I recommend it highly.

denny rydberg
President, Young Life (www.younglife.org)

Jim Burns has done it again! This is a practical, timely and reality-based resource for equipping teens to live life in the fast-paced, pressure-packed adolescent world of today.

rich van pelt
President, Compassion International, Denver, Colorado

Jim Burns has his finger on the pulse of youth today. He understands their mindsets and has prepared these studies in a way that will capture their attention and lead them to greater maturity in Christ.

rick warren
Senior Pastor, Saddleback Church, Lake Forest, California
Author of *The Purpose Driven Life*

jim burns

general editor

high school group study

winning
spiritual
battles

Published by Gospel Light
Ventura, California, U.S.A.
www.gospellight.com
Printed in the U.S.A.

All Scripture quotations are taken from the Holy Bible, New International Version®.
Copyright © 1973, 1978, 1984 by International Bible Society. Used by permission of
Zondervan Publishing House. All rights reserved.

© 2011 Jim Burns. All rights reserved.
Original material by Roger Royster.
Opening devotions for sessions written by Joey O'Connor.

Originally published as *The Word on Spiritual Warfare* by Gospel Light in 1996.

Uncommon high school group study & leader's guide : winning spiritual battles /
Jim Burns, general editor.
p. cm.
ISBN 978-0-8307-5836-4 (trade paper)
1. Spiritual warfare—Study and teaching. 2. Christian education of teenagers.
I. Burns, Jim, 1953- II. Title: Winning spiritual battles.
BV4509.5.U49 2011
235'.4—dc23
2011031766

Rights for publishing this book outside the U.S.A. or in non-English languages are
administered by Gospel Light Worldwide, an international not-for-profit ministry.
For additional information, please visit www.glww.org, e-mail info@glww.org, or write
to Gospel Light Worldwide, 1957 Eastman Avenue, Ventura, CA 93003, U.S.A.

To order copies of this book and other Gospel Light products in bulk quantities,
please contact us at 1-800-446-7735.

dedication

To Frank Trane

You have been a remarkable inspiration to my life and ministry. Frank, I have treasured every meal and conversation. Your energy and enthusiasm is contagious. Several years ago we had a conversation about spiritual warfare, and the end result is this curriculum for young people. You are loved and appreciated. Thank you for all you do for so many.

A Special thanks to Roger Royster for the great work you did on this project.

contents

how to use the *uncommon* group bible studies 9

unit I: prepare for battle

session 1: secure in salvation 13

session 2: transformed by Christ 29

session 3: a new identity in Christ 45

session 4: plugged in to God's power 61

unit II: understand your enemy

session 5: what spiritual warfare is all about 79

session 6: a profile of the enemy 95

session 7: the goals and weapons of the enemy 109

session 8: how to uproot the enemy's schemes 127

unit III: equip for the fight

session 9: wear your belt and protect your heart 143

session 10: put on your shoes and take up your shield 159

session 11: cover your head and swing your sword 175

session 12: contact the Commander-in-chief frequently 189

how to use
the *uncommon*
group bible studies

Each *Uncommon* group Bible study contains 12 sessions, which are divided into 3 stand-alone units of 4 sessions each. You may choose to teach all 12 sessions consecutively, to use just one unit, or to present individual sessions. You know your group, so do what works best for you and your students.

This is your leader's guidebook for teaching your group. Electronic files (in PDF format) of each session's student handouts are available for download at **www.gospellight.com/uncommon/winning_spiritual_battles.zip.** The handouts include the "message," "dig," "apply," "reflect" and "meditation" sections of each study and have been formatted for easy printing. You may print as many copies as you need for your group.

Each session opens with a devotional meditation written for you, the youth leader. As hectic and trying as youth work is much of the time, it's important never to neglect your interior life. Use the devotions to refocus your heart and prepare yourself to share with kids the message that has already taken root in you. Each of the 12 sessions are divided into the following sections:

starter
Young people will stay in your youth group if they feel comfortable and make friends in the group. This section is designed for you and the students to get to know each other better.

message

The message section will introduce the Scripture reading for the session and get students thinking about how the passage applies to their lives.

dig

Many young people are biblically illiterate. In this section, students will dig into the Word of God and will begin to interact on a personal level with the concepts.

apply

Young people need the opportunity to think through the issues at hand. This section will get students talking about the passage of Scripture and interacting on important issues.

reflect

The conclusion to the study will allow students to reflect on some of the issues presented in the study on a more personal level.

meditation

A closing Scripture for the students to read and reflect on.

unit I
prepare for battle

It was in the fourth grade that Roger's dad saved his life. For weeks he had been threatened, harassed and frightened by a kid from his neighborhood elementary school. The only reason Roger could find to justify this kid's behavior toward him was that he was the only kid in the class that was smaller than he was. That made Roger an obvious target for a preteen trying to affirm his growing manhood.

The two boys were fighting across the street from Roger's home. He had just plunged his fist into the garage door in a poor attempt to defend his honor against this bully. Like two bad dancers, they then did what many untrained preteen fighters do: fell to the ground and rolled across the cement in an effort to get a punch in here or there. Suddenly, the figure of a man appeared and quickly pulled apart the sparring partners. It was Roger's dad. *Where did he come from?*

Roger's dad held this kid high off the ground by his collar, and then placed him down just inches from his own feet. Looking him in the eye, he gave a huge karate-style "hey!" into his face. The yell was so shocking that it scared the fluids right out of this kid's body.

Roger's dad then stepped up to the bully and said, "I understand you have been threatening my son. Is this true?" The kid squeaked out a yes. "Well, the truth is," continued my dad, "when you mess with a child of mine, you mess with me. Now get out of here and don't bother us again." They had never seen a kid with wet pants run away so fast.

In Romans 8:31-32, Paul writes, "What, then, shall we say in response to this? If God is for us, who can be against us? He who did not spare his own Son, but gave him up for us all—how will he not also, along with him, graciously give us all things?" As you lead your students through this section, remind your students of how much the heavenly Father does to protect His children. Help them to understand that He is always on their side, supporting them in battle as they fight against the spiritual darkness that is in this world.

The truth is that all of us need to be intimately acquainted with our heavenly Father, who waits to give us loaves of bread, not bags of rocks (see Matthew 7:9). As you and your group work through this unit together, it is my prayer that the security of a life-changing Christ would become the source of strength that you and they need to stand strong against the enemy.

secure in salvation

The Lord is gracious and righteous; our God is full of compassion.
The Lord protects the simplehearted; when I was in great need, he saved me.
PSALM 116:5-6

As a youth worker involved with the critical task of shaping, nurturing and developing the lives of young people, you are a target for spiritual attack.

Now, before you get the willies, don't think that the devil lurks behind every 7-Eleven® Slurpee machine or that every misfortune or accident is caused by the devil himself. No, Satan is smoother than that. He is slick, calculated and deliberate. His schemes are designed to wreak the most havoc they can and impact as many lives as possible. That's why you and every person involved in active ministry are targets for his demonic work in this world. If you were a naval commander, would you go after individual planes or the aircraft carrier itself? Youth workers are like aircraft carriers deploying young Christians all over the world in various missions.

Lions don't stalk dead or diseased prey. In the same way, Satan, like a roaring lion (see 2 Peter 5:8), pursues living, active followers of Christ—those who are truly making a difference in this world for the kingdom of God. This is why it is so important for your group members to have a clear perspective on salvation. They can stand firm in the knowledge that they are children of God who have been saved by His grace. They are heirs of His kingdom!

Yes, your students are in a spiritual battle, and Satan will use the weapons at his disposal to try to destroy their relationship with God, their Commander-in-chief. However, they do not need to think of themselves as defenseless sheep surrounded by ravenous wolves, because God has promised to be their protector. Furthermore, they are fighting an enemy with limited power. Satan has limited abilities, limited resources and, best of all, limited time to wage his attacks!

Helping your students discover the security of their salvation in Christ is a wonderful gift to impart to them. When they are secure in their salvation, they will be in a position to firmly stand their ground against the enemy. They will know that they have all of God's unlimited firepower to fight off Satan's attacks. They will be indestructible targets who are willing to go on the offensive and fight back against the darkness that surrounds them in this world.

> *If salvation could be attained only by working hard,*
> *then surely horses and donkeys would be in heaven.*
> MARTIN LUTHER

secure in salvation

starter

ACT IT OUT: Make copies of the following "Act It Out" assignments (these are also available for download in pdf format). Divide students into three groups, and give each group a copy of one of the three situations. Allow students to have about seven minutes to read and discuss their group's situation.

After the groups have read their situation and discussed the two questions, have a volunteer from each summarize their answer to question 2 (or have two members from each group role-play the situation for the whole group). At this point in the session, don't focus on helping them answer question 2 correctly—just give them the opportunity to explore how well they understand what salvation means.

Note: You can download this group study guide in 8½" x 11" format at **www.gospellight.com/uncommon/winning_spiritual_battles.zip.**

act it out #1: katy and zack

Zack has been a Christian for five years and has just returned from camp. He finally understands what it means to experience salvation through Christ. One day, he is sitting reading his Bible when Katy walks up and sits down next to him.

"Zack, my life is a mess," Katy says to him. "I feel so lost. I wish I had something that would save me from my circumstances and change my life forever."

Discuss the following questions:

1. Katy needs to understand what salvation through Christ means and how it will change her life. How would you explain this to her?
2. What do you think Katy needs to know about salvation before she chooses to give her life to Christ?

act it out #2: liza and julia

Liza has quite a reputation around school for being worldly. Her parents are pretty wealthy. Liza has a nice car, nice clothes and plenty of spending money.

One day while having a conversation with Julia, Liza mentions that she is unhappy with her life. Julia and Liza know each other, but they have never been good friends. They first met in fifth-grade Sunday School back when Liza and her family went to church. Julia realizes that Liza needs to know Jesus and understand what it means to be saved by Him.

Discuss the following questions:

1. How would you explain to Liza the salvation that believers receive from Christ?
2. What do you think Liza needs to know about salvation before she chooses to give her life to Christ?

act it out #3: james and the coach

James is the shortstop on his school's baseball team, and all the players look up to him. One day, the baseball coach calls James into his office and asks him if he would be willing to share a team devotional and pray for the team before each game. James didn't even know that the coach realized he was a Christian. James and the coach begin to discuss what the team needs to know about salvation.

Discuss the following questions:

1. What are the important concepts a person needs to understand in order to experience salvation in Christ?
2. What do you think James needs to share about salvation before his team members will be able to choose to give their lives to Christ?

message

If you are a believer in Jesus Christ, you are engaged in a battle that is being waged each day on this earth. While you won't necessarily be able to see this battle—it is *spiritual* in nature—the struggle and your enemy, Satan, are very real. The reason you are under attack is because when you accepted Jesus into your life, you cancelled your allegiances with the kingdom of darkness and joined with God's forces in the kingdom of light.

Of course, Satan is not happy about losing you—and he certainly doesn't want to lose more because of your witness—so he will do whatever he can within his means to make you doubt that you really are a child of God. This is why having a clear understanding of what it means to be saved is so essential to living a victorious Christian life and overcoming Satan's attacks. Fortunately,

God's Word, the Bible, shows you exactly what salvation is, how it has been offered to you, and how it should affect your life.

what salvation is

Being saved means we are rescued from *something*. When a person first becomes a Christian, he or she is saved from sin and the eternal consequences of sin.

1. What does Ephesians 2:1 say is the result of living a life of sin?

    _____

    _____

    _____

    _____

2. Look up Romans 5:12 and 1 Corinthians 15:21-22. Through whom did we inherit spiritual death? How did it happen?

    _____

    _____

    _____

    _____

3. Who and what does Ephesians 2:2 say we were following before we accepted salvation in Christ?

    _____

    _____

    _____

    _____

how salvation is offered

Once we acknowledge our need to be rescued from sin, we need to understand how salvation is offered to us and how we can receive it.

1. Read Ephesians 2:4-5. Why does God want to make us
    alive with Christ even though we were dead in our sin?

    _____

    _____

    _____

2. In 1 John 4:8, we read that if we do not love, we do not
    _____ _____ because _____ ____

    _____.

3. Read Ephesians 2:8. What must we have to be saved?

    _____

    _____

    _____

4. From where does Ephesians 2:4-8 say the love, faith and
    grace we need for our salvation comes?

    _____

    _____

    _____

5. What does 1 John 1:8-9 say about how we can respond to
    God's love and grace? What does God promise to us in
    these verses?

    _____

    _____

    _____

how salvation affects our lives

Finally, we need to recognize how accepting God's gift of salvation will ultimately affect our lives.

1. Ephesians 2:8-10 says we are brought to a love-filled life for a reason. What is that reason?

   _____

   _____

   _____

   _____

2. Whose example does Ephesians 5:1-2 tell us we can follow?

   _____

   _____

   _____

   _____

3. How does this verse say we can imitate God?

   _____

   _____

   _____

   _____

dig

What is amazing about salvation is that the Bible says that God actually *seeks out* those who are lost. Rather than just sit back and wait for people to realize their condition, He actively engages them and calls them to come to Him. In Luke 15:1-32, Jesus told three parables to illustrate just how God seeks out those who are lost in sin. Read those parables and answer the questions that follow.

1. What was the attitude of the person seeking the lost item?

   _____

   _____

   _____

   _____

2. What was his or her response when what was lost was found?

   _____

   _____

   _____

   _____

3. What does this tell you about God's desire for people to be saved?

   _____

   _____

   _____

   _____

4. What is the first thing that comes to your mind when you hear the word "lost"?

   _____

   _____

   _____

5. What do you think it means when a person who does not know Christ is called lost (see Ephesians 2:1-2)?

   _____

   _____

   _____

6. What does it mean to you that before receiving salvation from Christ, you followed the ways of the enemy?

_____

_____

_____

_____

7. Read Ephesians 5:3-6. Listed below are some words from these verses that describe behaviors that are associated with a life of sin. Under each word list things that people do today to act out that sin.

Sexual Immorality

_____

_____

_____

Impurity

_____

_____

_____

Greed

_____

_____

_____

Obscenity

_____

_____

_____

Foolish Talk

_____

_____

_____

_____

Coarse Joking

_____

_____

_____

_____

8. The opposite of being lost is being found. What are things that must happen for something that is lost to be found?

_____

_____

_____

_____

9. How will a lost person who is seeking to be found feel about his or her sin? How is an awareness of sin and the need to escape its control a first step toward being saved?

_____

_____

_____

_____

apply

In Romans 3:23, Paul says that "all have sinned and fall short of the glory of God." Each of us is guilty of sinning against God, and none of us can escape the consequences of our actions. We are all trapped by our sin, much like the man in the following story:

> Many years ago, two men were canoeing down the Colorado River. At one point as they were leaving a dock, they accidentally maneuvered their canoe sideways in the current and capsized it. One of the men decided he was strong enough to hold the canoe, swim to the side of the river, and save all of their camping equipment.
>
> The man quickly realized his mistake when the rushing current pulled him, his belongings and the canoe back against the dock and down to the bottom of the river. He soon found himself 10 feet below the surface, pinned by the current between the canoe and the dock pilings.
>
> Up on the surface, the dock attendant frantically rushed around, looking for a way to keep the man from drowning. Spotting a green garden hose lying nearby, he picked it up and quickly began to lower it down to the bottom of the river. The drowning man saw the hose, grabbed it and began to breathe through it. Within 30 minutes, divers arrived and jumped into the water. They were finally able to free the man from the place where he was trapped and save his life.

1. What would you have done if you were the dock attendant?

----

2. If you were the man who was stuck, what would you have
   been thinking and feeling about your situation?

   ....
   ....
   ....

3. Spiritually, we find ourselves trapped in a similar circumstance in need of being rescued. What does Paul say in
   Ephesians 2:1-3 is the cause of our being trapped?

   ....
   ....
   ....

4. According to Ephesians 2:4-5, what saves us?

   ....
   ....
   ....

apply

God has provided a way for us to be saved from our sins so that
we can have fellowship with Him and one day spend eternity with
Him. Note that this salvation is a *gift*—we can't buy it or do anything to earn it, but we must accept it in order to receive it. Once
we have allowed God's life-giving love into our lives, we can stand
secure in our salvation. As Paul writes in Romans 8:38-39, "I am
convinced that neither death nor life, neither angels nor demons,
neither the present nor the future, nor any powers, neither height

nor depth, nor anything else in all creation, will be able to separate us from the love of God that is in Christ Jesus our Lord."

1. In these verses in Romans 8:38-39, Paul describes some things that separate an unsaved person from God. What type of challenges do you face in this world that attempt to come between you and God?

    _____

    _____

    _____

    _____

2. How does it make you feel to know that no matter what spiritual attack comes your way, nothing can separate you from God's love?

    _____

    _____

    _____

    _____

3. What are some things about salvation that you have a hard time understanding?

    _____

    _____

    _____

4. How can you find answers to your questions?

    _____

    _____

    _____

5. If you are a Christian, when and how did you come to understand the salvation you received from Christ?

----

6. What did it take (or would it take) for you to recognize that you need salvation through Jesus?

----

reflect

1. Someone once described a sin-filled life as "a life lived separated from God's life-giving love." What are some ways (outside of seeking God) that you have been tempted to meet your need for life-giving love?

----

2. How do you see your sin? (No big deal? A little out of control? Beyond forgiveness?)

----

3. Why is it important to see salvation as a gift? What choice have you made to respond to Jesus' offer of this gift of salvation?

_____

_____

_____

_____

4. If you have accepted God's gift of salvation, how has it affected your life? What difference has it made?

_____

_____

_____

_____

5. How does knowing that you can never be separated from God's love affect your relationship with the Lord? How does it affect the way you see yourself?

_____

_____

_____

_____

meditation

But because of his great love for us, God, who is rich in mercy, made us alive with Christ even when we were dead in transgressions—it is by grace you have been saved.

EPHESIANS 2:4-5

transformed
by Christ

I have set the Lord always before me. Because he is at my right hand, I will not be shaken. Therefore my heart is glad and my tongue rejoices.
PSALM 16:8-9

Transformation. The word is bold, powerful and dynamic. Transformation digs into the very soul of a person's longing for something new—a change, a new beginning. If it weren't for Christ's power to transform our lives, we would be living a completely lost, hopeless existence. Transformation is something every person needs on a daily basis.

New Christians, especially teenagers, often view transformation from an external perspective. They may not drink or do drugs anymore, may change their choice of music, may lose a few colorful adjectives from their vocabulary, and may treat others better than before they became Christians. However, there is more to transformation than just external actions. Transformation is not just a fixed event, a one-time prayer, or an instant change from a long life of sin and rebellion against God.

When believers are born into a new position in Christ and their faith begins to mature, they are challenged to seek daily transformation through the Spirit in the *inner life*. For new adolescent Christians, changing the outside might be relatively easy, but as they mature the Holy Spirit will want to get into the really tough stuff way down inside—serious matters of the heart such as will, pride, desires, thoughts, character, obedience and submission. These are the dark attics of our soul where Christ wants to crawl around for a while with His flashlight. It is the difference between a check-up and major surgery with the Master Physician. It's the kind of transformation that you, as an adult youth worker, probably couldn't have handled as a 16-year-old.

It's tempting to try to track our transformation by our performance. However, as a youth worker, you need to consider the inner transformation issues that God wants you to hand over to Him. Is your faith like many of the adolescents with whom you work, or does it reflect the Holy Spirit's obvious presence at this point in your adult journey of faith? Why such heavy questions, you ask? Before you begin teaching young people about transformation, it's critical for you to understand through your own experience that transformation begins from the inside out. Internal transformation will result in external change, but external transformation on its own will stop short. There is a critical difference.

After being born again a man experiences peace, but it is a militant peace, a peace maintained at the point of war.
OSWALD CHAMBERS

group study guide

transformed by Christ

starter

TRANSFORMERS: Get into four groups and take two minutes to list as many things that you can think of that change—a caterpillar to a butterfly, ice to water, a semi truck to Optimus Prime (just kidding). After two minutes, share the items on your lists with the other groups, and discuss the question that follows.

Note: You can download this group study guide in 8½" x 11" format at www.gospellight.com/uncommon/winning_spiritual_battles.zip.

How do the changes you listed illustrate the changes a person goes through when he or she comes to know Christ?

_____

_____

_____

_____

_____

message

When you turned your back on the sin of your past, accepted God's forgiveness and joined up with His forces, a transformation began to take place in your life. This process of change began the instant you accepted Christ, but it will take a lifetime to complete. It occurs through the power of God at work in your life, but you participate in it by cooperating with what God wants to do in you. Transformation is more than just going in a new direction—it means being re-created into a *completely new person.* It is essential for this change to occur if you want to stand strong against the attacks of your enemy.

a life-changing love
In John 3:16 we read, "For God so loved the world that he gave his one and only Son, that whoever believes in him shall not perish but have eternal life." It was because of God's love for us that He sent Jesus into the world to pay the price for our sin and transform us into new creations. As the following verses in Romans 8:1-15 demonstrate, this change brings about a profound difference in our motives, attitudes and actions.

Therefore, there is now no condemnation for those who are in Christ Jesus, because through Christ Jesus the law of the Spirit of life set me free from the law of sin and death. For what the law was powerless to do in that it was weakened by the sinful nature, God did by sending his own Son in the likeness of sinful man to be a sin offering. And so he condemned sin in sinful man, in order that the righteous requirements of the law might be fully met in us, who do not live according to the sinful nature but according to the Spirit.

Those who live according to the sinful nature have their minds set on what that nature desires; but those who live in accordance with the Spirit have their minds set on what the Spirit desires. The mind of sinful man is death, but the mind controlled by the Spirit is life and peace; the sinful mind is hostile to God. It does not submit to God's law, nor can it do so. Those controlled by the sinful nature cannot please God.

You, however, are controlled not by the sinful nature but by the Spirit, if the Spirit of God lives in you. And if anyone does not have the Spirit of Christ, he does not belong to Christ. But if Christ is in you, your body is dead because of sin, yet your spirit is alive because of righteousness. And if the Spirit of him who raised Jesus from the dead is living in you, he who raised Christ from the dead will also give life to your mortal bodies through his Spirit, who lives in you.

Therefore, brothers, we have an obligation—but it is not to the sinful nature, to live according to it. For if you live according to the sinful nature, you will die; but if by the Spirit you put to death the misdeeds of the body, you will live, because those who are led by the Spirit of God are sons of God. For you did not receive a spirit that makes you a slave again to fear, but you received the Spirit of sonship. And by him we cry, "Abba, Father."

1. According to this passage in Romans, what did God do for us? What response can we give that will allow God to transform our lives?

    _____

    _____

    _____

    _____

2. What is the difference between those who live according to the sinful nature and those who live according to the Spirit? What happens to each?

    _____

    _____

    _____

    _____

3. What type of transformation is illustrated by these verses? What type of promise have we been given if we embrace Christ's life?

    _____

    _____

    _____

    _____

4. How does God see us when we accept what He has done for us?

    _____

    _____

    _____

    _____

5. What type of spirit have we received? What does that mean in terms of what we should or should not fear?

----

6. How is transformation different from merely changing our behavior?

----

who we are in Christ

In 2 Corinthians 5:17, Paul states, "If anyone is in Christ, he is a new creation; the old has gone, the new has come!" When you accept God's forgiveness and join forces with His kingdom, your status changes in His eyes. You have a new identity and a new purpose, and God expects you to put off the things of the past and live as a child of the light. But what does this involve? In Ephesians 4:17-29, Paul provides the answer:

> So I tell you this, and insist on it in the Lord, that you must no longer live as the Gentiles do, in the futility of their thinking. They are darkened in their understanding and separated from the life of God because of the ignorance that is in them due to the hardening of their hearts. Having lost all sensitivity, they have given themselves over to sensuality so as to indulge in every kind of impurity, with a continual lust for more.

You, however, did not come to know Christ that way. Surely you heard of him and were taught in him in accordance with the truth that is in Jesus. You were taught, with regard to your former way of life, to put off your old self, which is being corrupted by its deceitful desires; to be made new in the attitude of your minds; and to put on the new self, created to be like God in true righteousness and holiness.

Therefore each of you must put off falsehood and speak truthfully to his neighbor, for we are all members of one body. "In your anger do not sin": Do not let the sun go down while you are still angry, and do not give the devil a foothold. He who has been stealing must steal no longer, but must work, doing something useful with his own hands, that he may have something to share with those in need.

Do not let any unwholesome talk come out of your mouths, but only what is helpful for building others up according to their needs, that it may benefit those who listen. And do not grieve the Holy Spirit of God, with whom you were sealed for the day of redemption. Get rid of all bitterness, rage and anger, brawling and slander, along with every form of malice. Be kind and compassionate to one another, forgiving each other, just as in Christ God forgave you.

1. What does it mean to "live as the Gentiles do"?

    _____

    _____

    _____

2. What does Paul remind us took place when we came to Christ?

    _____

    _____

    _____

    _____

3. Because of this, what types of behavior are we to put off?

_____

_____

_____

_____

4. How will these changes demonstrate that we are being transformed in Christ?

_____

_____

_____

5. What is God's part in this process? What is our part?

_____

_____

_____

_____

dig

As the process of transformation takes place in our lives and we begin to grow in righteousness (doing what is right) and holiness (being pure and set apart for God's purpose), we will start to reflect the nature and character of God. We will know that this change is taking place when we observe these three stages: (1) we begin to experience God's love in our lives; (2) we accept this love and begin to know God; and (3) that love allows us to love others. These three stages are demonstrated in 1 John 4:7-8:

Dear friends, let us love one another, for love comes from God.
Everyone who loves has been born of God and knows God. Who-
ever does not love does not know God, because God is love.

1. The first stage of our transformation is that we begin to
    experience God's love in our lives. What opportunity does
    God's love present in our lives?

    _____

    _____

    _____

    _____

2. What has to happen in our hearts for God's love to dictate
    how we treat others?

    _____

    _____

    _____

    _____

3. The second stage is that we accept this love and begin to
    know God. How does knowing God transform us?

    _____

    _____

    _____

    _____

4. How are loving others and knowing God connected?

    _____

    _____

    _____

    _____

5. In stage three, we begin to love others. Read 1 John 3:16. How is God's love different from the type of "love" that the world offers?

_____

_____

_____

_____

6. Take a look at the people in your group. What are some ways you have seen them transformed because of God's love?

_____

_____

_____

_____

apply

To stand strong against the attacks of the enemy, you must not only know your identity in Christ but also live as a member of God's kingdom. Unfortunately, because we live in "enemy territory," there are a lot of forces at work to keep us chained to our old lives so that we never see God's transforming power at work. The following story is about one such individual who experiences these types of stumbling blocks:

Derrick is 13 years old and has grown up in a non-Christian family. He recently attended a camp with some of his friends who attend a local church and made the decision to give his life to Christ. Derrick's parents think it is fine for their son to believe what he wants, but they don't consider themselves "religious" and don't want to hear him talk about God. Derrick hangs out with some friends who have not been the best influence on him, and he has been getting into a lot of trouble lately at school. Derrick's language and social activities reflect what his life has been like up until this point. He feels that God is calling him to do things differently—that He wants him to change—but Derrick feels he has no support and doesn't know where to begin.

1. Now that Derrick has accepted Christ, what are three immediate changes he needs to make to reflect his new status?

----

2. Given that Derrick has little support from his parents in his newfound faith, where can he go to get encouragement?

----

3. What daily habits does Derrick need to start so that he can begin to understand what it means to live as a Christian?

----

4. What changes can Derrick expect God to bring about as a result?

_____

_____

_____

_____

5. Christ came to change our lives completely. He desires to leave no area untouched, but He will not transform us without our cooperation. In each of the areas listed below, consider ways you need to be transformed by God's love so that you can be the person He has called you to be.

in your time . . .

_____

_____

_____

in your values . . .

_____

_____

_____

in your language . . .

_____

_____

_____

in your friends . . .

_____

_____

_____

in your music choices . . .

_____

_____

_____

in your interactions with your parents . . .

_____

_____

_____

in your actions at school . . .

_____

_____

_____

in your actions at church . . .

_____

_____

_____

in your overall attitude . . .

_____

_____

_____

6. Look at your list and consider one area in which you know
   you need to change. Write down one step you will take to
   give this area to God in the next week.

_____

_____

_____

7. What advice do the following verses have for those who want to grow and become like Christ—who want to live a transformed life?

Proverbs 3:5-6

_____

_____

_____

1 Thessalonians 5:16-18

_____

_____

_____

2 Timothy 1:13-14

_____

_____

_____

reflect

1. What are the three biggest areas of transformation that you have seen in your life this past year?

_____

_____

_____

2. What are three areas of your old life that have been the most difficult to put off?

_____

_____

_____

3. If a photo could be taken of your spiritual life today, what new changes would you see compared to a photo of your old life?

4. What are some specific roadblocks that need to be removed so that greater transformation can take place?

5. How has the work Christ has been doing in you given you the strength to resist temptations and other attacks from the enemy?

meditation

Put on the new self, created to be like God in true
righteousness and holiness.

EPHESIANS 4:24

a new identity
in Christ

I will praise the Lord all my life; I will sing praise to my God as long as I live.
Do not put your trust in princes, in mortal men, who cannot save.

PSALM 146:2-3

Bringing new life into the world is what makes youth ministry so exciting. As the teenagers in your group invite God into their lives, you are in the enviable position of observing their identity in Christ begin to grow and develop. Assisting your group members in this process is a privilege and a high calling, as those first few days, weeks and months will be critical to their faith development.

Why? Because Satan, "a liar and the father of lies" (John 8:44), will try to tempt your group members away from their new identity in Christ and unravel the work that God has done. Your love, support and encouragement will be crucial during this time to keep them on track. Just like a shepherd leading, protecting and guiding new lambs to safe pasture (see Psalm 23:2), assisting in the spiritual development of your teens will play a major role in their spiritual growth. God will actively work in and through you to minister to their needs.

Just as important—if not more important—in this process is for *you* to continually grow and develop your identity in Christ. Your teens are looking to you as an example of faith, and you can only share effectively what you have experienced personally. You need to be affirmed, encouraged, nurtured and inspired in your walk with Christ just as much as your young people do. So, right now, consider who is investing time and energy into you and your relationship with God. Who are your mentors—the people who encourage you? Who are your role models? Who do you go to for spiritual counsel and guidance?

For your sake—and your students' sakes—you need to be reminded about who you are in Christ. Sit down with a friend to read over some of the verses in this lesson and discuss how they impact your life. (Do this apart from preparing for the lesson!) Your birth in Christ was a life-changing event that you don't want to forget. Nurturing your identity in Christ is the only way to keep growing closer to Him.

The true center for self is Jesus Christ.
OSWALD CHAMBERS

a new identity
in Christ

starter

LET ME TELL YOU! Have the group members sit in a circle (if you
have a large group, form 2 or more circles) and give each person
an index card and a pen or pencil. Ask each student to write his
or her name at the top of one side of the card and then pass the
card to the person on his or her right. The person who received
the card is to write one or two words that describe a *positive* aspect
of the character of the individual whose name is on the card. After about 15 seconds, have students pass cards to the right again
and repeat the process. Continue as time permits, and then return the cards to their namesakes. When you are finished, have
each person consider the following questions:

Note: You can download this group study guide in 8¹/₂" x 11" format at
www.gospellight.com/uncommon/winning_spiritual_battles.zip.

1. According to your card, who do others think you are?

    ....

    ....

    ....

    ....

2. How would you describe the character of one you respect?

    ....

    ....

    ....

    ....

3. Why is that quality important to you?

    ....

    ....

    ....

    ....

message

From the beginning of creation, God's intention was to have a personal, loving relationship with people. He created a special place for Adam and Eve, the first humans, in the Garden of Eden and spent time with them. Unfortunately, it was there that Satan launched his first attack—and was successful at making Adam and Eve sin against God.

the original plan

Read the first part of the story from Genesis 1:27-31 and 2:15-25 that discusses God's original plan for humankind, and then answer the questions that follow.

So God created man in his own image, in the image of God he created him; male and female he created them. God blessed them and said to them, "Be fruitful and increase in number; fill the earth and subdue it. Rule over the fish of the sea and the birds of the air and over every living creature that moves on the ground."

Then God said, "I give you every seed-bearing plant on the face of the whole earth and every tree that has fruit with seed in it. They will be yours for food. And to all the beasts of the earth and all the birds of the air and all the creatures that move on the ground—everything that has the breath of life in it—I give every green plant for food." And it was so. God saw all that he had made, and it was very good. And there was evening, and there was morning—the sixth day. . . .

The LORD God took the man and put him in the Garden of Eden to work it and take care of it. And the LORD God commanded the man, "You are free to eat from any tree in the garden; but you must not eat from the tree of the knowledge of good and evil, for when you eat of it you will surely die." The LORD God said, "It is not good for the man to be alone. I will make a helper suitable for him."

Now the LORD God had formed out of the ground all the beasts of the field and all the birds of the air. He brought them to the man to see what he would name them; and whatever the man called each living creature, that was its name. So the man gave names to all the livestock, the birds of the air and all the beasts of the field.

But for Adam no suitable helper was found. So the LORD God caused the man to fall into a deep sleep; and while he was sleeping, he took one of the man's ribs and closed up the place with flesh. Then the LORD God made a woman from the rib he had taken out of the man, and he brought her to the man.

The man said, "This is now bone of my bones and flesh of my flesh; she shall be called 'woman,' for she was taken out of man."

For this reason a man will leave his father and mother and be united to his wife, and they will become one flesh. The man and his wife were both naked, and they felt no shame.

1. How did God see Adam and Eve?

    _____

    _____

    _____

2. How did Adam and Eve see themselves? How did they see each other?

    _____

    _____

    _____

    _____

3. Genesis 3:8 states, "Then the man and his wife heard the sound of the LORD God as he was walking in the garden in the cool of the day." Considering this description, how would you describe the relationship between Adam and Eve and God at this time?

    _____

    _____

    _____

    _____

the original plan is broken

So, God created a place for people to get to know Him and the opportunity to do so. The Garden of Eden was an environment where a loving relationship between God and people could thrive. How-

ever, for this love to be genuine, God wanted to give people the freedom to choose to love and obey Him—or not. The next part of the
story from Genesis 3:1-24 describes the choice that Adam and Eve
made and the role that Satan played in bringing this about.

*Now the serpent was more crafty than any of the wild animals the
LORD God had made. He said to the woman, "Did God really say,
'You must not eat from any tree in the garden'?"*

*The woman said to the serpent, "We may eat fruit from the
trees in the garden, but God did say, 'You must not eat fruit from
the tree that is in the middle of the garden, and you must not touch
it, or you will die.'"*

*"You will not surely die," the serpent said to the woman. "For
God knows that when you eat of it your eyes will be opened, and
you will be like God, knowing good and evil."*

*When the woman saw that the fruit of the tree was good for
food and pleasing to the eye, and also desirable for gaining wisdom, she took some and ate it. She also gave some to her husband,
who was with her, and he ate it. Then the eyes of both of them were
opened, and they realized they were naked; so they sewed fig leaves
together and made coverings for themselves.*

*Then the man and his wife heard the sound of the LORD God
as he was walking in the garden in the cool of the day, and they hid
from the LORD God among the trees of the garden. But the LORD
God called to the man, "Where are you?"*

*He answered, "I heard you in the garden, and I was afraid be-
cause I was naked; so I hid."*

*And he said, "Who told you that you were naked? Have you
eaten from the tree that I commanded you not to eat from?"*

*The man said, "The woman you put here with me—she gave
me some fruit from the tree, and I ate it."*

Then the LORD God said to the woman, "What is this you have done?"

The woman said, "The serpent deceived me, and I ate."

1. How did Satan, the serpent, play a part in pulling Adam and Eve away from God?

_____

_____

_____

_____

_____

2. Why did both Adam and Eve submit to this temptation?

_____

_____

_____

_____

3. What were the immediate results of their sin?

_____

_____

_____

_____

_____

4. How did Adam and Eve's choice affect the way they felt about God?

_____

_____

_____

_____

5. What reasons (excuses) did Adam and Eve give for disobeying God?

_____

_____

_____

_____

6. In Romans 12:12, Paul says, "Therefore, just as sin entered the world through one man, and death through sin, and in this way death came to all men, because all sinned." What impact did Adam and Eve's sin have on all of humankind?

_____

_____

_____

_____

the original plan restored

Fortunately, God did not leave humankind in that broken state. From the very beginning, He made a plan to restore and redeem the relationship that He had with Adam and Eve. Read the following words from the apostle Paul about how God accomplished His will on earth:

> For since death came through a man, the resurrection of the dead comes also through a man. For as in Adam all die, so in Christ all will be made alive. But each in his own turn: Christ, the firstfruits; then, when he comes, those who belong to him. Then the end will come, when he hands over the kingdom to God the Father after he has destroyed all dominion, authority and power. For he must reign until he has put all his enemies under his feet. The last enemy to be destroyed is death (1 Corinthians 15:21-26).

Once you were alienated from God and were enemies in your minds because of your evil behavior. But now he has reconciled you by Christ's physical body through death to present you holy in his sight, without blemish and free from accusation (Colossians 1:21-22).

1. What was restored for us today through the life, death and resurrection of Jesus?

    _____

    _____

    _____

    _____

2. What will be conquered at the end of time?

    _____

    _____

    _____

    _____

3. What is the last enemy to be destroyed?

    _____

    _____

    _____

    _____

dig

Since the time of Adam and Eve, a battle has been continually raging for the ownership of our souls. On the one side, God, our loving heavenly Father, wants us to be restored in our relationship with Him. On the other side, Satan and his minions want us to doubt God's love for us and turn our backs on Him.

1. In Revelation 12:9, we read that the serpent who tempted
    Adam and Eve is Satan and that he "leads the whole world
    astray." Based on the story you read in Genesis 3:1-24,
    what method does Satan use to pull us away from God?

    _____

    _____

    _____

2. Read Romans 6:23. What are the consequences when we,
    like Adam and Eve, choose to disobey God's commands?

    _____

    _____

    _____

3. Spiritual death is separation from God's love. According to
    Romans 6:23 and John 3:16-17, what did God do to defeat
    spiritual death and to restore our relationship with Him?

    _____

    _____

    _____

4. Read Ephesians 1:3-10. In this passage, Paul uses the state-
    ments "in Christ," "in Him," "through Him" and "in love"
    to describe how God responds to those who belong to Je-
    sus. What does He do for them? How does He see them?

    _____

    _____

    _____

5. In Christ we go from loveless orphans to beloved children of God the Father. We go from old lives to brand-new lives. As we place our trust in God's love for us and see ourselves as He sees us, we become transformed. This is *our new identity in Christ*. Read 1 John 3:1-3. How should those who belong to God see themselves?

----

apply

So, are you viewing yourself the way that God sees you? To find out, read each of the verses below out loud and then take a moment to consider how you are doing in that specific area. Then rate yourself on a scale from 1 to 10, with 1 being "I see myself through my lenses" and 10 being "I see myself through God's lenses."

1. I see myself as a brand-new creation (2 Corinthians 5:17):

1	2	3	4	5	6	7	8	9	10

I see myself through   I see myself through
my lenses   God's lenses

2. I see myself sealed by the Holy Spirit as a loved child of God (Ephesians 1:13-14):

1	2	3	4	5	6	7	8	9	10

I see myself through   I see myself through
my lenses   God's lenses

3. I see myself as a sanctified saint (1 Corinthians 1:2):

1	2	3	4	5	6	7	8	9	10

I see myself through   I see myself through
my lenses   God's lenses

4. I see myself as completely forgiven by God, holy and blameless (Ephesians 1:4):

1	2	3	4	5	6	7	8	9	10

I see myself through   I see myself through
my lenses   God's lenses

5. I see myself as Christ's ambassador (2 Corinthians 5:19-20):

1	2	3	4	5	6	7	8	9	10

I see myself through   I see myself through
my lenses   God's lenses

6. What are some things that can keep you from seeing yourself as God sees you?

7. What do you need to do or let go of to be a part of God's plan of restoration?

8. Many people are willing to see themselves as sinners, but many won't wear the title of "saint" (a forgiven sinner who seeks to put God first by trusting God with all he or she has and is). Why is seeing yourself as a sinner only selfish?

_____

_____

_____

_____

9. What is involved in being one of God's saints?

_____

_____

_____

reflect

It is your actions and attitudes that will ultimately demonstrate how you view yourself. Proverbs 3:5-6 states, "Trust in the LORD with all your heart and lean not on your own understanding," and when you trust in God's ways, you will see yourself for who you really are—His beloved child. This will bring victory into your life as you apply God's truths to your insecurities and trust Him to give you the strength to live out His plan.

1. What are three specific areas of insecurity in your life that influence the way that you act? Complete the following sentences:

I feel <u>like a failure</u>, so I <u>don't try new things</u>.

I feel _____, so I _____.

I feel _____, so I _____.
I feel _____, so I _____.

2. Let's take this list one step further. Fill in the blanks below for the same three insecurities, but this time apply the truth that you have learned about how you should see yourself given your new identity in Christ.

   I feel like a failure _____, so I don't try new things.
   However, God sees me as a success, so I shouldn't be afraid to venture out.

   I feel _____, so I _____.
   However, God sees me as _____, so I
   _____.

   I feel _____, so I _____.
   However, God sees me as _____, so I
   _____.

   I feel _____, so I _____.
   However, God sees me as _____, so I
   _____.

3. According to Romans 8:31-37, who is it that brings these insecurities? Who is on our side to combat these insecurities?

   _____
   _____
   _____
   _____
   _____

4. What are we as a result of our new identity in Christ?

5. How can you combat these insecurities and increasingly put your identity in Christ?

6. What do you see your friends basing their identities on? How can you encourage them to increasingly place their identity in Christ?

meditation

How great is the love the Father has lavished on us, that we should be called children of God! And that is what we are!

1 JOHN 3:1

plugged in to
God's power

Praise God in his sanctuary; praise him in his mighty heavens. Praise him for his acts of power; praise him for his surpassing greatness.

PSALM 150:1-2

A junior-higher once had the unfortunate and painful experience of discovering the power of electricity the hard way. One evening, he walked into the garage to get some clothes out of the dryer. On the cement floor next to the dryer was a small puddle of water. Remember this: water + a short circuit in a running dryer + bare feet = *Yeow!* The instant he stepped in the water and opened the dryer door, electricity came zapping up his arm like a bolt of white-hot lightning. It wasn't until his hair was standing up that his mind registered a panicked red alert. He jumped back from the dryer, screaming all sorts of high-voltage words.

The difference between getting zapped by static electricity and by the old dryer is equivalent to the difference between the power of the Energizer Bunny and a power station for a major U.S. city. In the same way, the difference between God's power and Satan's power is . . . well, there is no comparison.

Studying the power of God—wait . . . scratch that—*experiencing* the power of God is an awesome event in the life of a Christian. It's what makes this lesson on God's unlimited power so exciting. Knowing the power of God and how to get in touch with Him through prayer, studying Scripture and spending time with other Christians is what makes the truth of this lesson so important. Power brings confidence. Once your students understand and experience the unlimited power of God in their lives, they won't fear the limited power of Satan.

One of the best ways for teenagers to grasp the power of God is to hear about it in others' lives. Hearing one of their peers share how God has given him or her the strength to stop drinking or how to get along with his or her parents is a living demonstration of God's power at work. For young people to be convinced of God's power, they must see concrete changes in other peoples' lives and their own.

Why not take some time to reflect on God's power in your life? How has He demonstrated His power in your life lately? What kinds of changes has His power made? Letting young people see God's power at work in your life is a solid way to get His current running in their lives.

The Scriptures teach us the best way of living, the noblest way of suffering, and the most comfortable way of dying.

JOHN FLAVEL

plugged in to God's power

starter

THE POWER IS OUT: Gather three people together and share a story about when you have experienced one of the following situations:

- The lights went out in the house.
- Your car ran out of gas.
- The batteries died in your flashlight.
- You ran out of firewood for a fire.
- A candle you were using flickered out.
- You were sailing in the middle of a lake and the wind suddenly died down.
- You lost any type of power.

Note: You can download this group study guide in 8½" x 11" format at www.gospellight.com/uncommon/winning_spiritual_battles.zip.

1. When these things happened, how did you feel?

   ....

   ....

   ....

   ....

2. What did you need?

   ....

   ....

   ....

   ....

3. How would the "power outage" you described affect your ability to complete a necessary task?

   ....

   ....

   ....

   ....

message

Belonging to Christ means we have access to His power through the Holy Spirit. Maintaining a strong connection to Christ helps us to overcome any opposition we may face that attempts to derail our relationship with God.

standing strong

In 2 Timothy 2:6-9, Paul, speaking to a young pastor named Timothy, describes this power and encourages him to stand strong in Christ and pursue the life God intended for him. Read this passage, and then answer the questions that follow.

Fan into flame the gift of God, which is in you through the laying on of my hands. For God did not give us a spirit of timidity, but a spirit of power, of love and of self-discipline. So do not be ashamed to testify about our Lord, or ashamed of me his prisoner. But join with me in suffering for the gospel, by the power of God, who has saved us and called us to a holy life—not because of anything we have done but because of his own purpose and grace.

1. What does Paul instruct Timothy to do in this passage?

_____

_____

_____

_____

2. How does Paul describe the Holy Spirit?

_____

_____

_____

3. What purpose does God want Christians to pursue?

_____

_____

_____

_____

filled with power

In Ephesians 3:14-19, Paul prays that believers will have a strong power connection to God, and he describes how that power will impact their lives. Read through the following verses and circle the words that describe what believers can receive from God when they plug into Him as their power source:

For this reason I kneel before the Father, from whom his whole family in heaven and on earth derives its name. I pray that out of his glorious riches he may strengthen you with power through his Spirit in your inner being, so that Christ may dwell in your hearts through faith. And I pray that you, being rooted and established in love, may have power, together with all the saints, to grasp how wide and long and high and deep is the love of Christ, and to know this love that surpasses knowledge—that you may be filled to the measure of all the fullness of God.

1. What does Paul pray that God will do for the believers?

    ----

2. What does Paul pray the believers will do?

    ----

3. For what purpose does God give us His spirit?

    ----

plugging in to the source

Prayer is the means by which we talk with God. Just as having a heartfelt conversation with a friend will build a connection, having a genuine conversation with God and allowing Him to speak to you through His Word will build a relationship with Him. In the Bible, we read how Jesus knew God through His Word and spoke to Him frequently in prayer. On the night He was betrayed, Jesus was plugging into this "power source." The following account from Luke 22:39-46 describes His time of prayer and gives us some insight to His prayer connection with God:

> *Jesus went out as usual to the Mount of Olives, and his disciples followed him. On reaching the place, he said to them, "Pray that you will not fall into temptation." He withdrew about a stone's throw beyond them, knelt down and prayed, "Father, if you are willing, take this cup from me; yet not my will, but yours be done." An angel from heaven appeared to him and strengthened him. And being in anguish, he prayed more earnestly, and his sweat was like drops of blood falling to the ground. When he rose from prayer and went back to the disciples, he found them asleep, exhausted from sorrow. "Why are you sleeping?" he asked them. "Get up and pray so that you will not fall into temptation."*

1. According to this passage, Jesus was going to the Mount of Olives . . .

   ❑ For the first time
   ❑ Because His disciples were going and He decided to follow
   ❑ Because He had made a habit of doing so
   ❑ Because He heard someone was going to be arrested and He didn't want to miss it

2. Why did Jesus encourage His disciples to pray?

   _____

   _____

   _____

   _____

3. Jesus went to His Father to express His feelings and to receive the power to face His death on the cross. How did God respond to His Son?

_____

_____

_____

4. What did the disciples miss out on by not praying?

_____

_____

_____

_____

5. The Holy Spirit's power can help us do amazing things for God. Look up the following passages and describe what each says the power of the Holy Spirit can help us to accomplish. The first one has been done for you.

Ephesians 3:20
As believers we have the power to do immeasurably more than we ask or imagine.

John 14:12

_____

_____

_____

Ephesians 6:10-11

_____

_____

_____

Philippians 4:13

1 John 4:3-4

dig

We have access to great power through our connection to God
through Christ. We plug into this power by studying and obeying
God's Word, by having regular conversations with God in prayer,
and by connecting with others who belong to God's family. All of
these "power points" allow the Holy Spirit to empower us to accomplish the plans that God has for us. Let's look at each of these three
power points: (1) the Bible, (2) prayer, and (3) fellow Christians.

power point 1: the Bible

1. Read 2 Timothy 3:16. What does this verse tell us about the
   source of all Scripture—the "Power Book"?

2. For what does Paul say Scripture is useful?

3. In 2 Timothy 3:17, Paul calls a believer who plugs in through
    the Bible a "man of God." What will plugging in through
    the Bible do for us as believers?

    _____

    _____

    _____

    _____

power point 2: prayer

1. Read James 1:5-7. What does James say about prayer?

    _____

    _____

    _____

    _____

2. What does James say in verse 6 about why we do not al-
    ways receive what we ask of God?

    _____

    _____

    _____

    _____

3. What does James say in verse 7 about a person who doubts
    God will answer?

    _____

    _____

    _____

    _____

4. Read James 4:8-10. After telling us to always approach the
    Power Source with confidence, James goes on to encour-

age us when we have doubts that God is always listening. When we "come near to God," what is His response to us?

_____

_____

_____

power point 3: fellow Christians

1. Read Hebrews 10:23-25. Why do believers need a pack of power people around them?

_____

_____

_____

2. This passage also describes the kind of person who can be a positive power partner—an "energizer." What do energizers do for each other?

_____

_____

_____

3. Not all people are energizers. According to 1 Corinthians 15:33, what does an "energy eater" do in the life of a believer?

_____

_____

_____

4. What does Ecclesiastes 4:9-12 say about the benefits of having a power partner?

_____

_____

_____

apply

1. Connecting to God's power requires stepping out in faith, relying on the truth of His Word, being vulnerable with other believers, cultivating a prayer life and being willing to surrender your plans for God's greater plan. When you go to the Power Source in prayer, what is your level of trust? Rate yourself using the following scale:

---

1   2   3   4   5   6   7   8   9   10

Doubt God can   Believe God can

2. How can studying God's Word, the Bible, help you plug in to God's power?

3. It can be difficult to stay strong out there in the world, which is why having a pack of power people can help you get recharged for spiritual battle. What are some characteristics that help make your youth group a safe place where you can go to be recharged?

4. You can gain the strength to continue in difficult times by making a habit of going to the Father for power, just as Je-

sus did. What is one difficult circumstance you are facing in your family that needs God's power right now? How will you plug in to that power?

_____

_____

_____

5. If you struggle with asking for the Father's help, what will you do to make a habit of going to Him daily for strength?

_____

_____

6. What are several ways you can grow stronger in your relationship with Christ?

_____

_____

_____

7. Based on the list you made, what is one way to grow stronger in your relationship with Christ that you will do this week?

_____

_____

8. How can you be an "energizer" for someone else this week?

_____

_____

reflect

God's power will come into your life through His Holy Spirit working in your prayer time, Bible study and relationships with other believers. One way to make sure that you are always plugging in to this Power Source is to agree to take on the following commitments. As you read each commitment, ask God to help you follow through on what you decide to do. By doing this your life will never be the same—God will use you to fulfill His purposes and to impact others for Christ!

commitment 1: plug in to the Power Source

Your success in standing against the schemes of the enemy will depend on consistently plugging in to God, the Power Source. For this reason, the first commitment to make is to determine how many times each week you will read the Bible and pray.

I, _____, commit to forming a "weekly power connection plan" that will include:

- Plugging in to the Power Book (the Bible) each day
- Plugging in to the power point (prayer) each day

My plan is as follows:

- I will read the Bible __ times a week, at _____ A.M./P.M.
- I will pray _____ minutes each day, at _____ A.M./P.M.

Signed: _____ Date: _____

commitment 2: plug in to power partners

You need at least two "energizers" (committed Christians who can personally support you and encourage you to grow in Christ). One energizer should be someone your own age, while the second should be someone at least four years older than you. Make sure that the person is willing to hold you accountable to God and will commit to helping you stay properly connected to the Power Source. Also commit to spending time in prayer, Bible study and discussion with these people.

I, _____, knowing that my success in standing against the schemes of the enemy depends on plugging in to two power partners, commit to finding the following:

- An energizer my own age to be one of my power partners
- An energizer at least four years older (and wiser than me) to be my second power partner

My peer power partner is _____. We will meet together on _____ each week/month.

My older power partner is _____. We will meet together on _____ each week/month.

Signed: _____ Date: _____

---

commitment 3: plug in to power people

Now you need to consider who will be your "power pack people"—people you can turn to who will give you the support and encouragement you need.

I, _____, knowing that my success in standing against the schemes of the enemy depends on plugging in to a pack of power people, commit to making my youth group the most effective place possible to connect with God by serving my group. I will invest in my group in the following ways:

- _____
- _____
- _____

I commit to talking with my youth leader within one week from today about my commitments.

Signed: _____ Date: _____

meditation

I pray that out of his glorious riches he may strengthen you with power through his Spirit in your inner being, so that Christ may dwell in your hearts through faith.

EPHESIANS 4:16-17

unit II
understand your enemy

A counselor once told a group of students in a drug and crisis re-habilitation clinic the results of being called a radish. "The truth is," he said, "if I were to tell you each time I saw you—say five times a day—that you are a radish, you would eventually believe it. You would eventually get up in the morning, go to the mirror and see what you think is a radish."

One teen immediately responded, "No way. It is impossible to think you're a vegetable."

"Maybe so," the counselor replied, "but what if every time I saw you, I were to say you were worthless?"

At this point, a question from one of the girls in the group struck him. She asked, "What if it's the truth? What if you really are worthless?"

The counselor turned to her and said, "See, you proved my point. A person can easily feel worthless because of the many messages he or she receives. But people are not worthless—people *have* worth." From the look on her face, he could tell that the truth had hit home. Early in her life, her biological father had abandoned the family, only to later come back during her early teens and sexually molest her. She had spent a large part of her life searching for a lost love.

The Bible is clear about Satan's intentions: "The thief comes only to steal and kill and destroy" (John 10:10). Spend any time at all with a group of teens and it will soon become evident that an enemy is battling for their attention and their souls. I am convinced that educating your students in a balanced fashion about the truth of Satan and his demons is essential to their wellbeing. This section of the study will lead you on a journey to discover the enemy's desires, motivations and schemes.

However, we won't just leave you there. The Bible is also clear about God's plan to defeat Satan, sin and death. Christ has "come that they may have life, and have it to the full" (John 10:10). So, in this section you will also find victory in the power of a God who cares, and along with that victory comes abundant life.

God's best to you as you learn under the protection of a greater God.

what spiritual
warfare is all about

*You believe that there is one God. Good! Even the demons
believe that—and shudder.*

JAMES 2:19

It is annoying to be with a group of people who are talking about
a great movie you haven't yet seen. When it comes to knowing the
details of the film—what happens in the plot and what twists and
turns the story takes—you don't want to know a thing. You want
to see and experience the movie for yourself. You don't want to
know who dies, who wins, who loses or who makes off with the
money and the gorgeous girl who's ready to steal the money from
whoever made off with it. You want to make your own evaluation
of whether or not it was a good movie. You want to be surprised.

However, when dealing with spiritual matters, you *don't* want
to be surprised. Being surprised at the movies is fine, but on the

battlefield for our souls a surprise attack is the last thing you want. For this reason, understanding what goes on in the spiritual realms is absolutely necessary to walk with Christ. Why? Because if you ignore the spiritual forces of darkness, you are essentially leaving out a significant portion of life that Jesus encountered here on earth.

In the Bible, we read that Jesus faced Satan for 40 days alone in the desert (see Matthew 4:1-11; Mark 1:12-13; Luke 4:1-13). He cast demons out of a demonized man and commanded them into a herd of pigs (see Matthew 8:28-34). In fact, a large part of His healing ministry was spent casting out demons, and these demons recognized Him, called out His name and shuddered at His voice. At the final Passover meal, Jesus saw the work of Satan as he seized the heart of Judas and put events into motion that would eventually lead Jesus to the cross. Jesus faced these spiritual battles on a daily basis. As Christians, should we expect anything less?

As you spend time on campus or at church with teenagers, be aware of Satan's strategies against you, your ministry and the students themselves. This lesson will pull no punches. You and your students will receive good, solid information on what spiritual warfare is all about. You will find dozens of wonderful promises from God's Word to equip you to understand how to stand strong in Christ. And your students will learn the end of this exciting story—that in Christ, *we win* and Satan loses.

If we weren't capable of humbly depending on God for assistance, our
souls would be dragged down. Although this total dependence may sometimes
go against our human nature, God takes great pleasure in it.
BROTHER LAWRENCE

what spiritual warfare is all about

starter

THE ENEMY: For this activity, you will need a whiteboard and a dry-erase marker or a flip chart and marker. Ask your group members to think of how they would describe their enemy, the devil. Next, write the following acrostic on a whiteboard or flip chart. Ask the group members to complete the acrostic below using words they feel describe what Satan is like and how he acts.

D _____

E _____

C _____

Note: You can download this group study guide in 8½" x 11" format at **www.gospellight.com/uncommon/winning_spiritual_battles.zip.**

E ....

I ....

V ....

E ....

Read the following statement: "The more you know about the enemy, the better you will be at avoiding his influence in your life." Discuss with your group whether they agree or disagree, and why.

message

Whether we like it or not, we are engaged in spiritual warfare. Satan, the devil, is our enemy, and it is his intention to keep us from growing in Christ or drawing anyone else into a relationship with God. For this reason, we must understand the fight in which we are engaged so we can combat him effectively. Read the following "interoffice memo," and then answer the questions that follow.

Received: Yesterday 3:14 PM
From: Hark, the angel herald <hark@angelherald.com>
Re: Spiritual Warfare—What's It All About?

Staff writers,

There have been an unusual number of unexplained occurrences taking place in the Christian world. The word on the street is that it is something called "spiritual warfare." We need an article written on this, and you're the perfect team to write it. I've taken the liberty of providing you with some references from the Bible. They are in four groups, so you can divide them up if you prefer. Read the verses and write a response as directed, and then return to me.

group one: the battle taking place

1. Read the following Scriptures and write down what they have to say about the spiritual forces that exist in this world and the battle that is taking place:

Psalm 139:7-12

Luke 4:31-36

Romans 8:31-39

Ephesians 6:12-13

1 Peter 5:8

Revelation 12:10

----

2. When you have completed your research, write a paragraph
    or two summarizing what these verses say about the spiritual
    forces Christians battle and where these battles take place.

----

group two: the enemy's strategies

1. As you read the following Scriptures, write down what
    they have to say about the strategies the enemy uses to at-
    tack Christians:

Luke 4:1-13

John 8:43-44

John 10:10

_____

_____

_____

_____

Ephesians 2:1-2

_____

_____

_____

2. When you have completed your research, write a paragraph or two summarizing what these verses say about the strategies the enemy uses to attack Christians.

_____

_____

_____

_____

group three: the enemy's influence

1. As you read the following Scriptures, write down what they have to say about how the enemy's army tries to steal daily victories from believers:

John 10:10

_____

_____

_____

Romans 8:31-39

_____

_____

_____

Ephesians 2:1-5

_____

_____

_____

Colossians 1:21-23

_____

_____

_____

2. When you have completed your research, write a paragraph
    or two summarizing what these verses say about how the
    enemy's army tries to steal daily victories from believers
    and how the enemy actually hopes to influence us.

    _____

    _____

    _____

    _____

group four: the armies and weapons
1. As you read the following Scriptures, write down what they
    have to say about the two armies involved in this spiritual
    battle—who the commander-in-chief of each army is and
    what each commander's primary weapon is:

2 Chronicles 20:2-4,15-17

Luke 4:1-13,31-36

John 8:31-32,42-44

John 10:10

Romans 8:31-39

2 Corinthians 10:3-6

1 Peter 5:8

....

....

....

2. When you have completed your research, write a paragraph or two summarizing what these verses say about the two armies involved in this spiritual battle—who the commander-in-chief of each army is and what each commander's primary weapon is.

....

....

....

....

....

dig

It might be hard to imagine that there is a *battle* raging around you. After all, you don't see any signs of a physical struggle—things look pretty much the way they always have been. It's easy to dismiss the idea that spiritual warfare is actually real and that it has implications for you here on earth. However, the Bible tells us that you have an enemy, Satan, who is always on the prowl looking for ways to pull you away from God.

1. How can you know for sure there is a devil?

....

....

....

....

2. How does it benefit the devil to have people unaware of his activities?

3. What have you observed in your daily life that confirms there is a war taking place between the kingdom of God and the kingdom of darkness?

4. Consider the following list of how the Bible describes some of Satan's tactics. After each one, write a way you have seen this tactic in action.

Twisting the truth (see Genesis 3:1-5)

Playing on people's ignorance of God's Word (see 2 Corinthians 4:4; 1 John 4:1) and ignorance of Satan's tactics (see 2 Corinthians 2:10-11).

Tempting people to sin (see 1 Kings 22:22; Matthew 4:1-11)

Leading people astray (John 8:44-45; 2 Corinthians 11:3)

Encouraging disobedience to God (2 Corinthians 11:3; Revelation 12:9)

Keeping believers from growing in faith (Mark 4:15; 1 Thessalonians 2:18)

Stealing people's joy (2 Corinthians 12:7)

Accusing believers of sin (Zechariah 3:1; Revelation 12:10)

_____

_____

_____

_____

apply

Your enemy wants you to be ignorant of what he is doing so he can creep into your life in subtle ways. He wants to get you to the point where it feels like you are beyond God's help. God wants you to be armed for battle, with your eyes open and your heart strong, grounded in His Word and empowered by the Holy Spirit.

1. What tactics do you see the devil use most often to derail the faith of teenagers? (Consider how he might use things such as movies, TV, music, the Internet, sports, magazines, fashion, food, possessions, relationships, school and work.)

_____

_____

_____

_____

2. How have you seen the devil twist things that can be good, healthy or harmless into opportunities to pull a believer away from God?

_____

_____

_____

_____

3. In what ways have you experienced spiritual warfare?

4. How have you seen God defeat the devil's hold in someone's life?

5. Read 1 Peter 5:8. What are two action steps you can take
   to keep yourself from getting caught up in the evil of this
   present world?

6. What are the benefits of being able to identify the devil's
   efforts and take the offensive in the battle? How does God
   want to empower you to do this?

reflect

1. It is foolish to battle an enemy unarmed and unprotected. Where do you need the Holy Spirit to empower your spiritual life (prayer life, Bible study, healthy relationships with other Christians)?

_____

_____

_____

_____

_____

2. Read 2 Chronicles 20:15-17. How does the fact that "the battle is not yours, but God's" influence your concept of spiritual warfare?

_____

_____

_____

_____

_____

3. God is in charge of winning the battle, but you are called to stand your ground, resist the devil and not give him a foothold (a way to creep into your life by exploiting a personal weakness). Where are you most vulnerable to the devil's influence?

_____

_____

_____

_____

_____

4. How can you protect yourself in this area?

_____

_____

_____

_____

_____

5. Where do you see an opportunity to resist the devil and influence others to choose God?

_____

_____

_____

_____

_____

meditation

Submit yourselves, then, to God. Resist the devil, and he will flee from you. Come near to God and he will come near to you.

JAMES 4:7-8

a profile of
the enemy

How you have fallen from heaven, O morning star, son of the dawn! You have been cast down to the earth, you who once laid low the nations!

ISAIAH 14:12

You don't have to be in youth ministry too long before you realize what you've probably suspected for some time: the battle becomes more intense. Working with teenagers, families, volunteer staff and other youth workers will show you Satan's mission on earth: "The thief comes only to steal and kill and destroy" (John 10:10).

Some years ago, a youth worker asked, "If Satan were going to get you in one area, what would it be?" Ouch! Now, that's a good question. You can probably name more than one area. The truth is that we are all open to spiritual attack in one way or another. We are all vulnerable to Satan's ploys. His desire is to destroy our relationship with God, and he will use three primary means to do this.

First, he will discourage your spirit. Take a tired and discouraged youth worker and you'll find a plump, sitting duck for Satan's banquet table. Discouragement can close your heart to the voice of God and allow Satan to tickle your ears with whispers of deceit. He will get you thinking, *What's the use? None of these kids care. No one would notice if I wasn't here. I'm not making any kind of difference in these young people's lives.*

Second, Satan will discredit your ministry. It doesn't matter if you're a volunteer or paid youth minister, there will be problems, situations, conflicts and disagreements in your ministry that Satan will use to attempt to discredit your ministry. People will challenge your motives, point out your weaknesses, and draw battle lines against you. Satan will fire criticism at you in an attempt to attack your character and integrity. He doesn't care whether it's true or not, because he just wants to bring you down. He will do anything to pull your eyes off God and the work God has planned for you.

Third, Satan will distance you from God. Along with discouragement, Satan will needle you with disappointment and disillusionment to sever your friendship with Christ. Contrast this with Jesus' words in the second part of John 10:10: "I have come that they may have life, and have it to the full."

If you are feeling any of these emotions or conflicts, remember that you're not fighting against flesh or blood. Grab a friend to pray with you, and don't try to fight your battles alone. Always remember that Satan is a defeated enemy and that God has promised to give us the victory when we stand strong, equip our spiritual armor, and join together in repelling his attacks.

Prayer is the mortar that holds our house together.
St. Teresa

group study guide

a profile of
the enemy

starter

SHUT DE DO: Play a recording of Randy Stonehill's song "Shut De Do." This track, originally released way back in 1982, can be found on the album *Our Recollections* (released in 1996) and is available for download on Amazon or iTunes. As an option, you can also search for a video of others singing the song on YouTube (there are several versions available, including an acapella version at http://www.youtube.com/watch?v=fjGXhX4BAV0&feature= related). When everyone has heard the song or watched the video, discuss the following questions:

1. Who does the song say Satan is?

    _____

    _____

    _____

2. What do you think it means to "shut de do"?

    _____

    _____

    _____

3. What do you think it means to "light de candle"?

    _____

    _____

    _____

message

The ancient Chinese military general Sun Tzu (544–496 BC) taught his men the importance of knowing their enemy before going into battle. In *The Art of War*, he wrote, "If you know the enemy and know yourself, you need not fear the results of a hundred battles. If you know yourself but not the enemy, then for every victory gained you will also suffer.a defeat." In the same way, we as Christians need to be knowledgeable about our enemy, the devil. The following verses will help you create a profile of Satan based on his origins, personality traits and activities.

satan's origins

To begin to understand our enemy, we have to know his beginning and a bit of his background. The Bible is very clear about the Source from which all things originated:

For by him all things were created: things in heaven and on earth, visible and invisible, whether thrones or powers or rulers or authorities; all things were created by him and for him. He is before all things, and in him all things hold together (Colossians 1:16-17).

In the beginning God created the heavens and the earth. . . . God saw all that he had made, and it was very good (Genesis 1:1,31).

1. According to these verses, what things were created by God?

   _____

   _____

   _____

   _____

2. What does Paul say in Colossians about God's position in relationship to His creation?

   _____

   _____

   _____

   _____

3. What information do these verses give you about where Satan originated?

   _____

   _____

   _____

4. How did God view His original creation?

   _____

   _____

It's the age-old question: If Satan was a part of God's creation, and that creation was good, then how did he turn out to become an enemy of God? This is a question that scholars have wrestled with for years. Some theologians believe that Satan was God's greatest angel who went on a power trip and wanted to be like God. In his attempt at greatness, he led a revolt of angels in heaven and successfully tempted man in the Garden of Eden, scoring a heavy hit on God's love-filled plan. By going against God, he and his army of demons were cast out of heaven to dwell in darkness, as the following passages from the Bible relate:

> *How you have fallen from heaven, O morning star, son of the dawn! You have been cast down to the earth, you who once laid low the nations! You said in your heart, "I will ascend to heaven; I will raise my throne above the stars of God; I will sit enthroned on the mount of assembly, on the utmost heights of the sacred mountain. I will ascend above the tops of the clouds; I will make myself like the Most High." But you are brought down to the grave, to the depths of the pit* (Isaiah 14:12-15).

> *You were the model of perfection, full of wisdom and perfect in beauty. You were in Eden, the garden of God; every precious stone adorned you: ruby, topaz and emerald, chrysolite, onyx and jasper, sapphire, turquoise and beryl. Your settings and mountings were made of gold; on the day you were created they were prepared. You were anointed as a guardian cherub, for so I ordained you. You were on the holy mount of God; you walked among the fiery stones. You were blameless in your ways from the day you were created till wickedness was found in you. Through your widespread trade you were filled with violence, and you sinned. So I drove you*

in disgrace from the mount of God, and I expelled you, O guardian cherub, from among the fiery stones. Your heart became proud on account of your beauty, and you corrupted your wisdom because of your splendor (Ezekiel 28:11-17).

God did not spare angels when they sinned, but sent them to hell, putting them into gloomy dungeons to be held for judgment (2 Peter 2:4).

There was war in heaven. Michael and his angels fought against the dragon, and the dragon and his angels fought back. But he was not strong enough, and they lost their place in heaven. The great dragon was hurled down—that ancient serpent called the devil, or Satan, who leads the whole world astray. He was hurled to the earth, and his angels with him (Revelation 12:7-9).

1. What does the prophet Isaiah say was the main cause of Satan's fall?

   _____
   _____
   _____
   _____

2. List the five "I will" statements of Satan found in the Isaiah passage.

   I will _____
   I will _____
   I will _____
   I will _____
   I will _____

3. What does Ezekiel say about Satan in the beginning? What happened as a result of his sin?

    _____

    _____

    _____

4. What happened to Satan and his demons when they rebelled against the Lord?

    _____

    _____

    _____

5. Michael is referred to in the Bible as an "archangel," or chief angel (see Jude 1:9). He is the leader of God's angel army against Satan. Based on these verses, who is more powerful: God or Satan (see also 1 John 4:4)?

    _____

    _____

    _____

We don't know exactly how the devil went from being an angel, created by God, to being God's enemy. However, we do know that somewhere along the line, he made the choice to disobey God and put himself first. We also know that he is real and that he is a threat to the life that Christ has planned for Christians.

satan's personality

Scripture gives a number of different names for Satan, each of which describe an aspect of his character. Look up each of the following Scriptures and write down what it states about Satan's personality and/or his intentions toward God and people:

John 8:44

John 10:10

John 14:30

2 Corinthians 11:14

Ephesians 2:1-2

1 Peter 5:8

_____

_____

_____

Revelation 12:9-10

_____

_____

_____

dig

Who the enemy is dictates what he will do. In Satan's case, we know that his intentions are to keep people away from God and His love. He may not be able to win the war and override God's plan, but he is willing to take as many people down as he can before time runs out. Based on what you have learned about Satan and his intentions, finish each of the following sentences that describe Satan's influence in the world today:

1. Satan blinds unbelievers from knowing God by . . .

_____

_____

_____

_____

2. Satan deceives and pulls believers away from God by . . .

_____

_____

_____

_____

3. Satan uses lies and temptation to influence how people see God by . . .

_____

_____

_____

4. Satan makes evil look good by . . .

_____

_____

_____

5. Satan uses past sins to accuse believers, hoping they will . . .

_____

_____

_____

_____

6. Satan devours people like a roaring lion by . . .

_____

_____

_____

_____

apply

Sun Tzu once wrote, "Victorious warriors win first and then go to war, while defeated warriors go to war first and then seek to win." To effectively counter Satan's strategies and win spiritual battles, you need to not only know your enemy but also be prepared in how you will fight against his tactics.

1. Based on what you have read today, why is Satan a dangerous enemy?

   _____

   _____

   _____

   _____

2. How can people know when they see him?

   _____

   _____

   _____

3. How does knowing your enemy help you see his intentions and resist him?

   _____

   _____

   _____

4. What is evidence that you have seen of Satan's work in
   the world?

   _____

   _____

   _____

   _____

5. What can believers do to keep the enemy from messing up
   their lives?

   _____

   _____

   _____

   _____

6. Read Job 1:6-12. What does this passage tell us about the
   limits of Satan's authority on the earth?

7. How does this passage in Job demonstrate Satan's tactics
   in the world today?

8. Read Revelation 20:10. If Satan knows his ultimate fate,
   why do you think he continues to wage war against God?

Pray for one another's protection from the enemy's schemes.

reflect

1. What areas of your life are the most vulnerable to Satan's
   tactics?

2. How has he influenced the way you see yourself?

_____

_____

_____

3. What are some ways you can keep Satan from working his way into your life?

_____

_____

_____

4. How has he tried to interfere with your relationship with you and God?

_____

_____

_____

_____

5. How can your relationship with God become a weapon against Satan?

_____

_____

_____

_____

meditation

I have given you authority to trample on snakes and
scorpions and to overcome all the power of the enemy.

LUKE 10:19

the goals
and weapons of
the enemy

With your help I can advance against a troop; with my God I can scale a wall.
PSALM 18:29

Rock climbing is an activity in which you can be quickly humbled by the sheer size, height and power of the mountain you are traversing. It is also not an activity to be taken on lightly. From 1922 (the first year official records were kept) to 2011, more than 220 people have died scaling the heights of Mount Everest alone.[1] The cause of death in these cases ranges from altitude sickness to frostbite to falls to avalanches.

The Christian life is often like climbing a steep mountain. It is a journey marked by dangerous passes, difficult climbs and also safe stretches of peaceful pasture. The Bible warns us that

Satan lurks along the road of our journey and that he will use any tool, roadblock or pothole to distract us on our way. He will use any temptation, thought, event or circumstance to trip us up. Understanding this will equip both you and your students to know how to combat Satan's tactics and dirty tricks that might cause you to fall away from Christ.

Unfortunately, Satan has a scheme and a strategy for each one of us. However, while at times we may face difficult struggles and disappointing setbacks in our journey, we must remind ourselves to keep focused on the summit of the mountain and keep pressing toward the goal (see Philippians 3:14). God will use the setbacks we encounter to humble us and cause us to depend even more on Him. He will use the tests we experience to reaffirm His commitment to us as our heavenly Father.

God promises to protect us from all evil as we walk through the valley of the shadow of death (see Psalm 23:4). We are not on this journey alone. We can call on our Master and Commander at any moment and receive help in our time of need. We can turn to Him at any time throughout our day and experience His peace in our lives.

This truth is easy to forget when you are confronted with problems and challenges in your ministry. So, before you prepare for this lesson, spend some time alone with God thanking Him for His constant presence in your life. Remember that God has promised that He will never leave us or forsake us (see Deuteronomy 31:6). You are not alone on your journey, for Jesus is with you every step of the way.

The devil is a better theologian than any of us and is a devil still.

A. W. TOZER

group study guide

the goals
and weapons of
the enemy

starter

THE MOUNTAINEER: Before the meeting, print out a list of mountain climber's equipment from the Internet or some other source.[2]
When the meeting begins, hand out a blank piece of paper to
each person and have your group members take three to five minutes to list everything they think a mountain climber would need
to successfully complete a challenging climb. When everyone is
finished, review the lists, and then discuss the following questions as a group.

Note: You can download this group study guide in 8½" x 11" format at
www.gospellight.com/uncommon/winning_spiritual_battles.zip.

1. What research does an experienced climber need to do to prepare for a challenging climb?

2. What factors must be considered when planning a route?

3. What tools does a climber need to take to help him or her be successful in the attempt?

4. What circumstances might cause a climber to discontinue an attempt?

message

Experienced climbers who want to ascend a mountain will draw on their extensive knowledge to plan a route that promises the best odds of reaching the top. They will use whatever methods and tools they have at their disposal to achieve their goal and be victorious over the mountain. In the same way, Satan will use his tools and extensive knowledge of our weaknesses to plan the most effective strategy to pull us away from God and damage our relationship with Him.

satan's prime targets

Satan isn't content with just keeping unbelievers from becoming Christians (see 2 Corinthians 4:4). He also specifically targets Christians and does everything he can to make them doubt God, avoid growing in their faith, and turn their backs on God. Although he can't be everywhere and doesn't know everything that God does, he receives a lot of help from the demons that serve him (see Revelation 12:7-8). In John 15:18-25, Jesus reveals why Christians are such intriguing targets for Satan:

If the world hates you, keep in mind that it hated me first. If you belonged to the world, it would love you as its own. As it is, you do not belong to the world, but I have chosen you out of the world. That is why the world hates you. Remember the words I spoke to you: "No servant is greater than his master." If they persecuted me, they will persecute you also. If they obeyed my teaching, they will obey yours also. They will treat you this way because of my name, for they do not know the One who sent me. If I had not come and spoken to them, they would not be guilty of sin. Now, however, they have no excuse for their sin. He who hates me hates my Father as well. If I had not done among them what no one else did, they would not be guilty of sin. But now they have seen these miracles, and yet they have hated both me and my Father. But this is to fulfill what is written in their Law: "They hated me without reason."

1. What did Jesus mean when He said that the world hated Him and that it will hate us?

2. According to this passage, to whom do we belong?

3. Why would that make Christians intriguing targets for Satan to conquer?

4. Based on Jesus' words, what treatment can we expect to receive from the world?

5. What do these attacks indicate about which side we serve?

satan's five main tools

There are five main tools Satan uses to wage his attacks on believers: (1) deception, (2) accusation, (3) weaknesses, (4) temptation, and (5) our sin nature. We will examine each of these in turn.

1. *Deception:* Mountain climbers will use a special hammer to remove debris from the rock, make handholds or foot-holds, or drive wedges deep into the stone to create a more climbable surface. Deception can work like a climber's hammer, creating an opening for Satan to get a firm footing in our lives. Read each of the Scriptures below and write what they say about the kinds of deception Satan uses to pull believers away from God:

Genesis 3:2-5,13

_____

_____

_____

_____

Matthew 24:23-24

_____

_____

_____

_____

Romans 1:25

_____

_____

_____

_____

2.   *Accusation:* Climbers will use a pick to open up
cracks in the rock and create a place to hammer
in climbing wedges, which will then aid them in
traversing difficult areas. In the same way, Satan uses accusations to open up old cracks and wounds that have been
healed by God, which then aid his efforts to create doubt
and conflict in our lives.

Read Revelation 12:10: How can constant accusations affect our faith?

_____

_____

_____

Read John 8:3-11: How does the accuser work through
people in this story?

_____

_____

_____

Read James 4:7-8,11-12: What attitudes accomplish Satan's purposes?

_____

_____

_____

3.   *Weaknesses and strongholds:* After climbers open up
weak spots in the rock with a pick, they will attach a climbing clip in the crack and use those

clips to create a more solid foothold. In the same way, once Satan exposes our weak areas, he will use those weaknesses to establish a stronghold.

Read 2 Corinthians 10:3-5. What weaknesses does Satan exploit and turn into places that he can have an influence in our lives?

Read Matthew 16:21-23. What evidence of a stronghold in Peter's life do we see in this encounter?

----

4. *Temptation:* Climbers thread ropes through climbing clips to secure themselves and their tool bags to the face of the mountain. These ropes keep them secure and locked into place and prevent them from falling. In the same way, Satan uses his rope of temptation to lasso us away from God's plans and keep us locked into the stronghold he has created. Read the following verses and write what they tell us about this particular technique of Satan:

1 Timothy 6:9-10

James 1:13-16

---

5. *Our sin nature:* Climbers are greatly aided by natural foot-holds that they come across in the face of a mountain. Unlike digging holes or exposing cracks, these natural footholds, which have been a feature of the rock for generations, provide instant access for the climber to use to reach his goal. In the same way, Satan uses our natural tendency to sin as an easy foothold to achieve his greater goals. Read the following verses, and then identify some of these specific footholds Satan uses in our lives:

James 4:1-3

James 4:4-8

---

1 John 3:7-10

---

dig

1. What result does Satan hope to see when he uses the tool of deception (see Matthew 24:24)?

   ....

   ....

   ....

   ....

2. What accusations does Satan make against us? What does James 4:7-8 say we can do when the enemy attacks us?

   ....

   ....

   ....

   ....

3. Read 2 Corinthians 2:5-11. What does Satan know will be the ultimate outcome when believers don't forgive someone who has hurt them?

   ....

   ....

   ....

   ....

   ....

4. Why is forgiveness an important part of foiling Satan's agenda?

   ....

   ....

   ....

   ....

5. A common stronghold with which both believers and non-believers struggle is the thought that God could never forgive them for what they have done. This can keep them from trusting God for their future, prevent His love from filling them, and affect their ability to forgive others. What does Romans 5:8 tell us about the truth of God's love?

_____

_____

_____

6. According to James 1:13-16, from where does temptation come?

_____

_____

_____

7. What result does Satan hope temptation will achieve (see 1 Timothy 6:9-10)?

_____

_____

_____

8. What are some natural footholds common to all believers that Satan uses to conquer us?

_____

_____

_____

apply

1. Why do you think the enemy goes to so much trouble to divert a believer's attention from God?

   _____

   _____

   _____

   _____

   _____

2. How have you seen the enemy successfully lure another believer away from a growing relationship with Jesus?

   _____

   _____

   _____

   _____

3. What are some obvious deceptions that believers struggle with daily?

   _____

   _____

   _____

   _____

   _____

4. What are some common accusations and lies believers struggle with on a daily basis?

   _____

   _____

   _____

   _____

5. What are some of the common temptations with which
   believers struggle? What hope does Paul offer to us in
   1 Corinthians 10:12-13?

   _____

   _____

   _____

   _____

   _____

6. Pride, greed and inappropriate expressions of anger are
   some examples of natural footholds that the enemy uses
   to get a good grip on believers. There may also be deeper
   generational footholds—such as alcoholism and abuse—
   that make it even easier for Satan to achieve his goals.
   What are some other natural footholds that you see in
   people's lives (see Ephesians 4:25-32)?

   _____

   _____

   _____

   _____

   _____

reflect

The following story is about a girl named Susan and a common
situation that many teens may face on a daily basis. Read the
story and then answer the questions that follow.

Susan and her friend Jane were making their way home
from school. Before she had left her house that morning,
Susan's mom had asked her to come right home and

watch her younger brother so she could attend a meeting. However, when Susan walked past a local ice cream shop, she saw a group of people she recognized from school sitting there.

"Look, Susan," said Jane, "there's Mandy, Amber and Tiffany from school. Why don't we go inside and meet them?"

"I can't," said Susan. "I promised my mom I would go right home from school."

"Well," said Jane, "it's not like you are going out of the way—this is on the way home. I'm sure your mom wouldn't care if you stepped in for just a minute. Besides, these girls are really popular, and it would be awesome if people saw us all hanging out. And your mom doesn't want you to be unpopular, does she?"

Susan had struggled with feelings of not fitting in at school, so the idea of possibly being seen with the "in" crowd appealed to her. "I . . . I suppose it's okay if we go in for just a minute," she said.

Thirty minutes later, Susan and Jane left the ice cream shop. "I've got to go!" Susan said to Jane. "I'm late. My mom is going to kill me!"

When Susan arrived home, her mom was waiting for her. "Where have you been?" she said. "I told you to come home right after school!"

"I . . . well, Jane needed some help . . . and it took a bit longer than I expected," Susan lied.

This excuse seemed to appease her mom. "Well, next time be more punctual when I ask you to come home at a certain time," she said. She picked up her car keys. "I'll be back in two hours."

Susan felt awful after her mom left. *Well, I did it again,* she thought. *Why can't I just tell the truth? Now I've disobeyed and lied about it—again. Some Christian I am. I'll never be free from this.*

1. How did Satan use the hammer of deception in this story?

2. How did he use the pickaxe of accusation?

3. How did he use the climbing clips of weaknesses and strongholds?

4. How did he use the rope of temptation?

5. How did he use the footholds of people's sin nature?

_____

_____

_____

_____

6. Thinking back over what you've learned during this session, identify one scheme the enemy is using to rope you into moving away from God.

_____

_____

_____

_____

7. What two footholds or influences have you allowed to remain in your life? What can you do to remove them?

_____

_____

_____

_____

8. Just as godly traits can be passed down from a parent to a child, there are also generational footholds or sins that can be passed down. What are some attitudes or behaviors in your family that are open doors to the devil's influence?

_____

_____

_____

9. It is encouraging to know that even though the enemy has substantial power, he is no match for God. What passages have you read during this session that will help you the next time you encounter Satan's schemes?

_____

_____

_____

_____

_____

meditation

No temptation has seized you except what is common to man. And God is faithful; he will not let you be tempted beyond what you can bear. But when you are tempted, he will also provide a way out so that you can stand up under it.

1 CORINTHIANS 10:13

Notes
1. "List of Deaths on Eight-thousanders," Wikipedia.org. http://en.wikipedia.org/wiki/List_of _deaths_on_eight-thousanders.
2. For one option, see the list of mountain climber gear *Backpacker Magazine* has posted on its website at http://www.backpacker.com/mountaineering_gear_checklist/gear/12101.

how to uproot the enemy's schemes

See to it that no one takes you captive through hollow and deceptive philosophy, which depends on human tradition and the basic principles of this world rather than on Christ.

COLOSSIANS 2:8

On board every U.S. Navy warship is a special room called the Command Intelligence Center, or CIC for short. The CIC is the place where Navy warships track both friend and foe through sophisticated radar. The main purpose of the CIC is to protect the vessel from incoming attacks, and technicians can track the movement of ships, planes and submarines from hundreds of miles away. The CIC is the first line of defense to warn the ship's crew of any incoming missiles or torpedoes. In times of war, the reliability of the CIC could mean the difference between life and death for the crew.

As Christians, God has given us our own Command Intelligence Center. Our CIC is the Holy Spirit at work in us—the spiritual radar we use to detect the oncoming attacks of Satan. The Holy Spirit guides our thoughts, motives and attitudes by transforming our minds with the mind of Christ (see Romans 12:2). Because of God's power within us, we are able to discern and test every thought (see 1 John 4:1). The more we grow in the knowledge of God's Word, the more we can fill our minds with His truth in order to discover how He wants us to live (see 2 Peter 3:17-18).

Our minds are the seedbeds of our actions. If Satan can fill our heads with negative thoughts, destructive thinking and guilt-filled anxiety, His work will soon influence our actions. If we harbor jealousy, envy, lust, doubt, hatred, bitterness or any other secret sin in the dark hidden corners of our minds, it will only be a little while before our lives will produce the fruit of our flesh. However, when we understand how Satan tries to attack our minds with his lies and deceit, we can use the power of God's Word to develop a defense system that he will never be able to penetrate.

What areas of your mind are the most vulnerable to Satan's attacks? How are you filling your mind with God's Word? How has God's Word helped you to discern the fiery lies of your enemy? Think about these questions as you prepare this lesson. Allow the presence of God to fill your mind as you seek to impact the lives of young people for eternity. Remember that no matter what the enemy attempts to do in your life, you are a son or daughter of the King. Jesus Christ's death and resurrection sealed the defeat of Satan, and you can rest assured in the hope of your salvation.

Sin has many tools, but a lie is the handle that fits them all.
ANONYMOUS

how to uproot the enemy's schemes

starter

ONE THING LEADS TO ANOTHER: Complete the following sentences. Share your responses with someone else, and then discuss the questions that follow.

When I think of the first day of school, I feel _____

_____

and it makes me want to _____

When I think of my best friend, I feel _____

_____

and it makes me want to _____

When I think of my worst enemy, I feel _____

_____

and it makes me want to _____

When I think of falling in love, I feel _____

_____

and it makes me want to _____

When I think of the struggles I face, I feel _____

_____

and it makes me want to _____

1. How does a feeling lead to an action?

_____

_____

_____

_____

2. What other feelings often lead to an action?

_____

_____

_____

_____

3. What determines if the action is positive or negative?

_____

_____

_____

_____

message

Satan knows that tempting you to sin and turn away from God begins with your mind. Thoughts are the beginning of feelings, and feelings motivate actions—both good and bad. He knows that if he can plant a thought in your head that is contrary to God's truth, he might be able to influence your feelings and pull you into sin.

recognizing the weeds

The following parable, adapted from Matthew 13:24-30, illustrates just how Satan works in our lives. Personalize the parable by writing your name in the blanks.

The kingdom of heaven is like a farmer named _____ *who planted good seed in his (or her) field. But while everyone was sleeping,* _____ *'s enemy came and planted weeds among the flowers and went away. When the flowers sprouted, the weeds also appeared. At first the farmer couldn't tell the difference between the flowers and the weeds until the flowers formed buds.*

_____ *'s servants came to him (or her) and said, "*_____*, didn't you plant good seed in your field? Where then did the weeds come from?"*

"An enemy did this," _____ *replied.*

The servants asked him, "Do you want us to go and pull them up?"

"No," _____ *answered, "because while you are pulling the weeds, you may uproot the flowers with them. Let both grow together until the harvest. At that time I will tell the harvesters: First, collect the weeds and tie them in bundles to be burned; then gather the flowers and bring them into my warehouse."*

1. The field in this parable represents your life, and you are the farmer. According to this parable, you have two things growing in your field. What are they?

   ....

   ....

   ....

2. Where did the weeds come from?

   ....

   ....

   ....

3. When were the weeds planted? What could the farmer have done to prevent the weeds from taking root?

   ....

   ....

   ....

   ....

4. Why didn't the farmer recognize the weeds when they first sprouted?

   ....

   ....

   ....

   ....

5. What was the ultimate fate of the weeds?

   ....

   ....

   ....

   ....

staying grounded

If we are grounded in God's Word, we will be able to recognize Satan's schemes before they can take hold in our lives. The Bible is filled with advice on how we can recognize this evil for what it is and strike back against it before it takes root.

1. Read 1 Thessalonians 5:12-22. Why does Paul ask the believers to "live in peace with each other" and "warn those who are idle"?

2. Why is it important to be joyful always, pray continually and give thanks in all circumstances? How does this help us defeat Satan's attacks?

3. Read Romans 12:1-3. What standard should we use to measure if something is good or evil?

dig

As the "farmer" of your life, you have the responsibility to create a healthy environment where God's Word can be planted and your relationship with Him can grow strong.

1. What are five things you can do to grow "healthy" flowers? (For example, thank God for what He does for you.)

    ----

2. What are five ways a farmer can create an unhealthy environment for growing flowers? (For example, gossiping.)

    ----

3. Often, people try to "be good" or deal with their sin on their own. However, the Bible is clear that without tapping into God's power through the Holy Spirit, any effort to root out sin in your own power will be futile. Read Romans 8:13-16. How does the Holy Spirit help you to overcome your sin nature?

    ----

4. The battle against the enemy's schemes will begin in your mind long before it shows up in your behavior. This is why Paul says in Romans 12:2 that you are transformed by the *renewing* of your mind. Read Philippians 4:8. How does this verse say you can replace "weeds" with "flowers"?

    ----

5. What is at least one thing you can think of that falls into each of the categories listed in Philippians 4:8: true, noble, right, pure, lovely, admirable, excellent and praiseworthy?

6. How can you replace negative thoughts planted by the enemy with those that will transform your mind according to God's will (see Romans 8:13; 12:2)?

7. As God's child, you are part of a family filled with many brothers and sisters. How can being part of this family environment—with God at the center—help you to stand strong against the enemy?

apply

The following story is about a girl named Jackie. Jackie is a victim of a scheme of the enemy that has left her doubting the existence of God (or at least doubting that He is a loving God). As you read this story, identify how Satan has been able to attack her faith and lead her to her present condition.

Jackie was born into an alcoholic family. Her dad abandoned the family when she was six years old. He didn't come back into the picture until Jackie was about 10. When he returned, he tried to reestablish a relationship with Jackie, but her mom didn't trust him, so she wouldn't allow it. Finally, her mom slowly let Jackie's dad back into her life.

When Jackie turned 12 years old, her dad sexually abused her and then disappeared again. At 14, Jackie had a relationship with an older boy that became sexual as well. After about a month, he left her brokenhearted.

Jackie has a warped sense of reality. She is searching for the love she never got from her dad in the relationships she builds with guys, but she is unhappy, hopeless and hurting. Jackie believes that if God had never made her, she wouldn't have been molested. She believes ultimately the mess that her life has become is all God's fault.

1. What events was the enemy able to orchestrate that were outside of Jackie's control?

_____

_____

_____

_____

2. What decisions did Jackie make that contributed to her present situation?

_____

_____

_____

_____

3. How did the enemy use these events to twist the truth and lead Jackie to believe that it was all God's fault?

_____

_____

_____

_____

4. If Jackie asked you for help, what would you tell her?

_____

_____

_____

5. Jesus' parable in Matthew 13:24-30 implies that flowers are the good thoughts and behaviors that make us better and keep us closer to God. We want to nurture these types of thoughts and allow them to grow. But the weeds—bad thoughts and behaviors (sin)—attempt to choke out these flowers and keep us from maturing in Christ. What are two flowers people your age might have growing in their field?

_____

_____

_____

_____

6. What are five specific things teens can do to grow godly things in their lives? (For example, hang out with affirming people who love God.)

_____

_____

_____

7. What are five things teens can do to kill a good life? (For example, hang out with people who encourage bad behavior and attitudes.)

_____

_____

_____

_____

8. How do you determine which things help you grow stronger and which do not?

_____

_____

_____

reflect

Once the enemy has sown weeds into our field, it takes a plan of attack to get them out. It is Christ's desire to set us free from all our weeds. As Jesus says in John 8:31-32, "If you hold to my teaching, you are really my disciples. Then you will know the truth, and the truth will set you free." Holding on to Jesus' teaching can be hard work as you attempt to change wrong behaviors and work at renewing your mind. However, with the Holy Spirit's help, you can see the lies behind Satan's schemes and witness God's love and power in your life. The result will be freedom in your life.

1. What is a struggle you are going through that has left you feeling hurt, angry, resentful, anxious or depressed?

_____

_____

_____

2. What specific thoughts or feelings has that struggle produced within you?

3. What behaviors did you act out as a result?

4. What deception was involved in your reaction, thoughts or attitudes? (For example, *I can't do anything right; I can't trust anyone; no one really loves me; the only safe thing to do is escape; I am worthless.*)

5. What biblical truth or truths can you plant in place of this weed as you pull it from your life?

6. Who can give you godly support as you go through this process?

_____

_____

_____

_____

_____

7. Write a prayer to Jesus committing this transformation to Him and asking Him to guide you as you get used to planting new flowers in your life.

_____

_____

_____

_____

_____

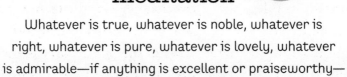

meditation

Whatever is true, whatever is noble, whatever is
right, whatever is pure, whatever is lovely, whatever
is admirable—if anything is excellent or praiseworthy—
think about such things.

PHILIPPIANS 4:8

unit III
equip for the fight

Imagine a young couple two weeks away from receiving the gift of a baby. They know that it will be a boy, because they were able to tell during the ultrasound test. Like many first-time parents, they stared at the screen looking for signs of health and life. Their first glimpse of anything recognizable was the top of the baby's head, and they only knew that because the technician told them. It all looked like shades of gray, until suddenly out of the darkness in the upper right corner of the screen came the wave of a tiny little hand. One, two, three, four fingers and a thumb.

When we consider this new life, we can be convinced of two things. First, the same God who has this baby boy's undivided attention within the womb will feel a bittersweetness the day the child is born. Today, there is nothing to distract this baby from intimacy with God, our Creator. But on the day he is born, an onslaught of needs and stimulation will infiltrate his life and distract him from God.

The second thing of which we can be sure is that the same God longs for the day His intimacy with this son will be restored through intimacy with His Son. And with that rebirth will come another kind of armor designed to protect all of God's children from the distractions the enemy sends our way. As Paul writes, this is spiritual armor that will allow him to "take [his] stand against the devil's schemes" (Ephesians 6:11). As Paul goes on to explain, this armor consists of several parts:

- The belt of truth
- The breastplate of righteousness
- The shoes of the gospel of peace
- The shield of faith
- The helmet of salvation
- The sword of the spirit

In this unit, we will look at God's armor and some practical ways to wear it. As you go through this material with your group, challenge your students to grasp the value of this information. They need to know that the armor of God provides them with much-needed protection and equipment as they travel through this earthly life.

Thank you for caring enough about your group members to equip them for victory.

wear your belt and protect your heart

Let your eyes look straight ahead, fix your gaze directly before you.
Make level paths for your feet and take only ways that are firm.

PROVERBS 4:25-26

Most teenagers love amusement parks. Six Flags® Magic Mountain, a wild Southern California amusement park known for intense rides such as the Viper, Colossus, Dive Devil, Ninja and Revolution, the world's first 360-degree looping coaster ever built, offers the ultimate extreme ride experience.

One summer, a high school ministry headed out for a day of death-defying, stomach-dropping, head-spinning, throat-clutching, white-knuckler rides. After making it through long, slow lines at the most popular rides, they climbed into the coasters where their bodies were suddenly thrown into a volatile series of torquing twists, spins and drops equal to that of a NASA astronaut training program. They quickly learned to appreciate the mysterious, powerful forces of speed, gravity, thrust and motion.

Although the forces associated with roller coasters are largely invisible when you're zipping down a 100-foot drop and heading into two successive loops followed by a few corkscrew turns, you're plenty glad to be strapped in by a secure seatbelt. Spend any time at an amusement park and no one will have to convince you of the physical manifestation of unseen forces. What is true of the physical world is equally true of the spiritual world. You need to be strapped in tight!

This chapter will strengthen you and the students in your ministry by teaching them how to strap on the belt of truth and the breastplate of righteousness. As Paul tells us in Ephesians 6, the spiritual forces we fight against are invisible, unseen and deceptively wicked. We need to be strong in the Lord and His mighty power. Our strength is dependent on His strength, so we must yield our will and our power to His.

Perhaps you've been feeling discouraged lately, as if you are trapped on a giant roller coaster of negative situations. Have you perhaps forgotten that you're in a spiritual battle zone and that there are invisible forces out to crush you like a chest-compressing 3g turn? This is why prayer is such an essential element to strapping on the belt of truth and the breastplate of righteousness.

Be strong in His power and rest in His grace. Although you may feel like you're on an unending roller coaster, fighting powerful, unseen forces, the truth is that Jesus is sitting in the seat right next to you.

When Jesus comes in, the shadows depart.
AUTHOR UNKNOWN

wear your belt and protect your heart

starter

BRING IN REINFORCEMENTS: For this activity you will need three volunteers. Choose the strongest guy or leader you have, one of your smallest students, and another somewhat bigger guy. Ask the smallest volunteer to stand in front of the group. Tell that student that you are going to test his or her strength and balance by having one of your bigger guys try to push him or her off balance. The volunteer's job is to resist the pressure by pressing back against the bigger guy with his or her shoulder. Ask your bigger guy to gently, but firmly, use a shoulder to push on the volunteer until he or she loses footing. (Be clear that this is the only action

Note: You can download this group study guide in 8½" x 11" format at **www.gospellight.com/uncommon/winning_spiritual_battles.zip.**

allowed—no poking, tickling or other contact.) Repeat this one or two more times, and then ask the group the following questions:

- Why wasn't our volunteer able to stand against the strength of the bigger guy?
- What does our volunteer need to overcome the strength of the bigger guy?

After hearing several suggestions, ask your strongest guy or leader to come up and stand between the two students with the smallest student behind him. Ask the bigger guy to try to push both your strongest guy and the smallest student off balance. The smallest student may push on the back of the strongest guy. Stop the game once the point is clear that adding the strongest guy was a great advantage for the smallest student. Allow time for students to share the difference they observed between the two situations.

message

The enemy is powerful, but followers of Christ have the advantage of God's greater power and protection from Satan's attacks. In Ephesians 6:10-13, Paul states exactly what believers are up against and what they have been given to protect themselves:

Finally, be strong in the Lord and in his mighty power. Put on the full armor of God so that you can take your stand against the devil's schemes. For our struggle is not against flesh and blood, but against the rulers, against the authorities, against the powers of this dark world and against the spiritual forces of evil in the heavenly realms. Therefore put on the full armor of God, so that when the day of evil comes, you may be able to stand your ground, and after you have done everything, to stand.

1. Where are believers told to find their strength?

2. What does a believer need to do to receive strength?

3. To whom does the armor belong? How much of the armor do we need to wear?

4. What is the result of putting on the full armor of God?

5. What words does Paul use to describe our enemy?

the belt of truth

Every piece of God's armor is important. In Ephesians 6:13, Paul begins to list these pieces in order, beginning with the belt of truth. Note that when Paul wrote these passages, he was under house arrest and guarded by Roman soldiers. Each piece of armor and equipment was very familiar to him—he saw it on his guards every day—as well as to his readers.

1. Read Ephesians 6:13. In Paul's day, people wore loose clothing. A belt wasn't specifically a piece of armor, but it played an important part in preparing a soldier to put on his armor. The fact that it was "buckled" tells us that it was tightly secured around the waist. How would a belt be an important article of clothing for a soldier?

    _____

    _____

    _____

2. The belt is described as "truth." Write down what the following verses say about God's truth and how it prepares us to stand against the enemy.

    Psalm 51:6

    _____

    _____

    Psalm 86:11-12

    _____

    _____

John 8:31-32

_____

_____

_____

_____

John 14:6

_____

_____

_____

Jesus is truth, and wrapping Him close around us like a belt allows us to have His wisdom and understanding. Truth is the foundation that prepares us when confronted with the enemy's tactics of lies and deception.

the breastplate of righteousness
Once we have truth firmly in place, Paul tells us to put "the breastplate of righteousness in place" (Ephesians 6:14). A breastplate is a piece of defensive armor. Worn in its proper place, it shelters the heart and other vital organs from injury.

1. Why would a breastplate be important to a soldier in battle? What might the consequences be for leaving this piece of armor behind?

    _____

    _____

    _____

    _____

2. The breastplate is described as "righteousness." The word "righteous" can be defined as "acting in accord with divine or moral law: free from guilt or sin."[1] Write down what the following verses say about where righteousness comes from and how it protects us from the enemy.

Romans 3:22

_____

_____

_____

Romans 5:17-19

_____

_____

_____

Romans 6:17-18,22-23

_____

_____

_____

Righteousness implies not only right action but also right character. Simply doing what is right leaves a hole in the armor. Jesus *is* the "truth" (see John 14:6) and the "righteousness of God" (see 2 Corinthians 5:21).

dig

Roman soldiers who went into battle together fought in very close-knit groups. Each man thought of the next soldier as his brother, which was why Roman soldiers rarely if ever fled from battle. For the soldier, running from battle was equivalent to letting down his family, which would have been unbearable to him. The soldiers stayed in ranks and fought together regardless of the odds. In the same way, as Christians in God's army, we are to join with our fellow spiritual fighters and confront the enemy head on. We are to never run from a fight (notice that Paul does not list any armor in Ephesians 6 to protect our backs), but draw strength from our fellow believers and attack.

1. Paul wasn't kidding when he said in Ephesians 6:10 to "be strong in the Lord and in his mighty power." What mental and physical characteristics does a strong Christian soldier have?

2. Describe the battlefield on which the Christian is fighting—the arenas of life that the enemy is challenging. Keep in mind that our battle is against the *spiritual forces of evil*, not the people who are caught up in that evil. Where should we focus our efforts of resistance?

3. What does it mean for us as Christians "to stand our ground" or "stand firm" (see Ephesians 6:13-14)?

4. Why is truth an essential element for the Christian's armor?

_____

_____

_____

_____

5. According to John 8:12, what advantage is given to people who follow Jesus?

_____

_____

_____

_____

apply

As Christians, we are instructed to put on the belt of truth first because it is the foundation for our relationship with Christ. In 1 John 1:5-10, we read in greater detail how we can power up our belt of truth:

> *This is the message we have heard from him and declare to you: God is light; in him there is no darkness at all. If we claim to have fellowship with him yet walk in the darkness, we lie and do not live by the truth. But if we walk in the light, as he is in the light, we have fellowship with one another, and the blood of Jesus, his Son, purifies us from all sin. If we claim to be without sin, we deceive ourselves and the truth is not in us. If we confess our sins, he is faithful and just and will forgive us our sins and purify us from all unrighteousness. If we claim we have not sinned, we make him out to be a liar and his word has no place in our lives.*

1. What is the result of having truth tightly bound around our waist as we stand against the attacks of the enemy?

2. What does it mean that "God is light"? What does it mean to "walk in the light"?

3. What happens when we walk in the light?

4. What happens when we claim to be without sin? According to this passage, what does this make Jesus out to be?

5. Once we equip the belt of truth, we then receive the breastplate of righteousness. In 1 John 2:3-6, we see how truth

becomes righteousness as shown by our obedience to Christ, and how that obedience is evidence of the truth in our hearts:

We know that we have come to know him if we obey his commands. The man who says, "I know him," but does not do what he commands is a liar, and the truth is not in him. But if anyone obeys his word, God's love is truly made complete in him. This is how we know we are in him: Whoever claims to live in him must walk as Jesus did.

According to these verses, how do we know we are "in" Jesus?

_____

_____

_____

_____

6. What is the relationship between knowing the truth and living in righteousness?

_____

_____

_____

_____

7. In Matthew 5:14, Jesus calls believers "the light of the world." What are some ways that Christians act as a light in this spiritually dark world?

_____

_____

_____

_____

8. If we focus our battle against the enemy, and not the people caught in the enemy's schemes, what impact can the light in a Christian's life have on those who are in darkness?

    _____

    _____

    _____

    _____

9. In Matthew 5:14, Jesus calls believers "the light of the world." What are two ways another Christian has been a light for you?

    _____

    _____

    _____

    _____

reflect

As Christians, we are in a battle against a very real enemy, and equipping the belt of truth and the breastplate of righteousness will be an important part of our success. Read each of the following situations. As you do, consider how you can stand firm with truth and righteousness close at hand and reach out to those who are vulnerable to the enemy's schemes.

Hamby was raised in a Christian home and attended church throughout high school. When he went to college, he took a course in evolutionary biology and then one in geology. As he attended these classes, he began to believe that he had been trusting a very old book (the Bible) when he should have been trusting some very new science. After this, Hamby took a course in ethics and began to believe that he had been following a system in which God was an authoritarian, holding a stick over his head. He made a commitment that day to do the right thing "just because it's the right thing to do."[2]

1. What would you say to a person like Hamby about the source of truth?

2. How does Hamby's story reflect the way in which Satan deceives people?

Jack is not a Christian but is concerned about doing the right thing. He has been dating his girlfriend for six months and has strong feelings for her. This Saturday she has invited him over to her house for their six-month anniversary dinner. Although Jack's girlfriend has not come right out and said she wants to sleep with him, she has dropped some big hints. Jack needs some advice, so he goes to his best friend, Tom. Tom has been a strong Christian for six years and actually broke up with a girlfriend over the same issue.

3. What would you say to Jack if you were Tom? How would you convince him to wear the breastplate of righteousness in this situation?

4. What areas of your life do you need to bring into the light of truth?

5. What would it mean for you to experience freedom in these areas?

6. What is one way you need to be more obedient to God's Word?

7. In what ways does your heart need the protection of God's righteousness?

    _____

    _____

    _____

    _____

    _____

8. What are two ways you can be the light of God's truth for someone today?

    _____

    _____

    _____

    _____

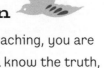

meditation

Jesus said, "If you hold to my teaching, you are
really my disciples. Then you will know the truth,
and the truth will set you free."

JOHN 8:31-32

Notes
1. "Righteous," Merriam-Webster online dictionary. http://www.merriam-webster.com.
2. Adapted from Alex McFarland, *10 Answers for Skeptics* (Ventura, CA: Regal, 2011), pp. 49-50.

session 10

put on your
shoes and take up
your shield

The Word became flesh and made his dwelling among us.
We have seen his glory, the glory of the One and Only, who came from
the Father, full of grace and truth.

JOHN 1:14

Have you ever spoken with a student who was hung up on trying to figure out what they believe? Ever faced a teenage interrogator in one of those yeah-but-what-about-this conversations? Every youth ministry is filled with a number of inquisitive students who are asking, seeking, postulating, theorizing and attempting to honestly dig into the mind of the Almighty. Perhaps God purposely puts at least one student like this in every youth group just to keep the adult leaders on their toes. Who knows? Perhaps in 10 to 20 years, these kids will be leading theologians.

159

It is important to know what you believe. Knowing God's Word and the truth of historical Christianity are powerful assets in warding off Satan's attacks on your heart and mind. However, with all that said, knowing what you believe isn't as significant as knowing in whom you believe. God did not send a "what" to die on a cross for your sins—He sent a "who," a Person, His only Son, Jesus Christ. Christianity is a who, not a what.

With the constant help of the Holy Spirit, we can meet Jesus every day by discovering who He is in His Word. By applying what we learn about who we believe in, we can grow in His grace and wisdom. This is just one of many ways to develop the faith of young believers. Your students' perplexing questions, ranging from the evolution of dinosaur brains to the existence of a pet heaven to whether or not Jesus hung out at a 7-Eleven as a teenager are vital to their faith and intellectual development. And if it's important to them, then it should be important to you.

One thing you will want to be sure to do is to steer your group members back into the direction of a Savior with dusty sandals, sweat on His brow, hands that healed and eyes filled with tears— God in human flesh. Grasping, knowing and experiencing the living Jesus is much more satisfying and intimate than knowing archaeological facts, Temple measurements and Bible maps. Only by knowing Jesus—this real man from Nazareth—will you and your students be able to experience peace and victory. Jesus is not just something in which we believe, but in *whom* we believe.

We need the power that comes from being certain that God is there, so sure of
His love that we can work on in confidence at the task before us.
GLORIA GAITHER

put on your shoes and take up your shield

starter

SOLDIER WITHOUT ARMOR: For the following skit, you will need two volunteers to read the parts of the sergeant and the soldier. The soldier should be wearing just pants and a shirt—no shoes, jacket or hat. Have three or four other volunteers join in as "extras." If you have access to props for the soldier in the skit, place the following nearby just off-stage: a belt with a buckle, a leather vest and tall boots. If you do not have access to these props, write the following in large print on self-adhesive paper and cut apart: "belt," "breastplate," "tough shoes." Also, get a piece of cardboard

Note: You can download this group study guide in 8½" x 11" format at **www.gospellight.com/uncommon/winning_spiritual_battles.zip.**

and write the word "tank" on it (you can also cut it out in the shape of a tank if you like). Ask one volunteer to read the part of the sergeant and the other the part of the soldier (the extras can just stand facing the sergeant). The soldier should act out the action described as quickly as possible, putting on the pieces of armor mentioned or applying the word for the armor to the part of the body where it would be worn.

Sergeant: All right, men. I have a dangerous mission and need a volunteer.

Soldier: I'm ready, Sarge! What do you want me to do?

Sergeant: As you know, the main attack will come from the north side. I need you to approach from the south and allow yourself to be seen.

Soldier: But if they see me, they're going to shoot me.

Sergeant: That's the idea. While you are diverting their fire, we'll catch them unawares.

Soldier: Okay! I'm ready! When do we start?

Sergeant: As soon as you're ready.

Soldier: I'm ready now, Sarge! I'm off.

Sergeant: Hold it!

Soldier: Changed your mind, Sarge? Decided I was too important to risk?

Sergeant: No, it's just that I see you've got a lot of equipment. How will you carry it all?

Soldier: No problem! All my equipment fits onto my belt. It's here, around my—oh. No it isn't . . . oh, I remember. I took it off in the tent while I was resting. Half a minute. I'll run and get it. [*Exits and quickly puts on belt.*]

Sergeant: [*To himself*] And he wonders if he's expendable. [*To the group*] Okay, men. Listen up. When he comes back, he'll be heading south. Now, we'll split up into three sections . . .

Soldier: [*Enters.*] Ready now, Sarge! I'm off! Wish me luck!

Sergeant: Wait a minute! We're supposed to be prepared. Now, what's going to happen when the enemy spots you?

Soldier: They'll be so overcome with fear that they'll all run away?

Sergeant: Guess again.

Soldier: They'll shoot at me?

Sergeant: Right! And what will happen if a bullet strikes you in the chest?

Soldier: Nothing, Sarge. It will bounce harmlessly off of my bulletproof vest.

Sergeant: What vest?

Soldier: The one that I'm wearing. [*Looks.*] The one I'm *not* wearing. Where did I leave it? Oh, I remember. When we stopped to make camp, I saw some blueberries. I didn't have a bucket to collect them, so I used my vest. It's over at the mess hall. Wait here. I'll be right back. [*Exits and quickly puts on vest.*]

Sergeant: Okay, men. Let's go over the plan one more time. James and John, you'll command the other two sections. If anything happens to me, then, Peter, you'll take over the third section . . .

Soldier: [*Enters.*] I'm back. And I'm off.

Sergeant: Wait. Before you go . . . what sort of terrain will you be going through?

Soldier: Train? I'm not taking the train.

Sergeant: Not "train." I said "terrain." That's the territory, the ground, the land. What will it be like?

Soldier: Well, there are rocks and thistles and thorns . . .

Sergeant: And how will you get across that terrain without hurting your feet?

Soldier: Are you kidding? These army boots are the finest made. Nothing can penetrate their soles.

Sergeant: What boots?

Soldier: The ones I have . . . where? What did I do with my boots? Wait, I remember! When we stopped, my feet were tired and sore. So I took off my boots and swished my feet in the river—don't go away. I'll be back. [*Exits and quickly pulls on boots.*]

Sergeant: [*To himself*] That's what I'm afraid of. [*To the group*] Okay, men. Now, James and John, you'll have to select an alternate from your section to replace you as leader in case something happens . . .

Soldier: [*Enters.*] Ta da! I found them. I'm ready to go!

Sergeant: Now, hold on. What will happen if someone from the other side lobs a grenade at you? I can't have you being all blown up and messing up the mission.

Soldier: Whew! That's quite a relief, sir!

Sergeant: You need something to shield you.

Soldier: But I don't have anything like that. What do I do?

Sergeant: Well, why don't you climb into that tank over there.

Soldier: Eh . . . sir?

Sergeant: Yes, certainly you've taken the basic course in tank warfare, right?

Soldier: Was that a required course, sir?

Sergeant: Well, nothing to be done about it now. You'll have to climb in there and just do your best. There's really nothing to it.

Soldier: Okay, sir. I'm off like a bunny!

Sergeant: [*To himself*] He'll never be ready, and he's got no chance of driving that tank without training. [*To the group*] Time for a new tactic! Let's go, men! [*Sarge and the extras exit.*]

Soldier: [*Enters walking backward with the "tank" sign or cutout.*] Okey-dokey, Sarge, I think I'm getting the hang of this. Ready when you are . . . whoah! [*Drives off the stage, maybe even crashing into something.*][1]

message

Being unprepared for battle is a ticket to failure. You need all of the armor of God, and you need to know how to equip it and use it correctly. Read the following passage from Ephesians 6:13,15-16. As you do, consider the role that footwear and a shield play in protecting a soldier from danger.

> *Therefore put on the full armor of God, so that when the day of evil comes, you may be able to stand your ground, and after you have done everything, to stand . . . with your feet fitted with the readiness that comes from the gospel of peace. In addition to all this, take up the shield of faith, with which you can extinguish all the flaming arrows of the evil one.*

shoes of the gospel of peace

A Roman soldier wore "grieves," which covered the lower part of his leg and allowed him to walk unhurt by anything sharp or dangerous on the path. He also wore heavy sandals with metal nails in the bottom. These sandals helped him keep his footing on uneven or slippery ground and brace himself against the enemy's brute force.

1. With what should the feet of the believer be fitted?

2. The word "gospel" means good news. What do the following verses tell us about the good news that God gives us?

    John 3:16-17

    1 John 4:10

    1 Peter 3:18

3. How does this news bring peace?

the shield of faith

The shield a Roman soldier carried was made of wood covered in leather. When held in place, it would cover most of the soldier's body. The Roman troops could also connect their shields together to form a wall—giving the troop strength in numbers. (This was known as the *testudo*, or "tortoise," formation.) The leather on the shield protected the wood underneath from the fire arrows that the Romans' enemy often shot. These arrows flew swiftly, were difficult to anticipate, and wounded the soldier deeply when it found its mark. Fire, like poison, inflicted additional damage.

1. What name is the shield given in Ephesians 1:16?

   _____

   _____

   _____

   _____

2. Hebrews 11:1 describes faith as "being sure of what we hope for and certain of what we do not see." How does being sure of—or having confidence in—our shield help us stand against the enemy?

   _____

   _____

   _____

   _____

3. What do the following verses say are the results of faith— of confidently believing that Jesus, God's Son, died and rose from the dead to take away our sin?

John 10:10

_____

_____

_____

_____

Romans 6:1-11

_____

_____

_____

_____

1 Thessalonians 5:10

_____

_____

_____

_____

Hebrews 9:15

_____

_____

_____

_____

4. How do peace and faith work together to help a soldier do his or her job effectively?

_____

_____

_____

_____

5. What effect does the shield of faith have against the arrows of the enemy?

_____

_____

_____

_____

dig

If you are a Christian, you are an essential part of a larger group of revolutionaries who are fighting for what is rightfully yours. Jesus willingly sacrificed His very life to win the battle for your freedom. When He rose from the dead, He delivered the final blow to defeat death—the enemy's greatest weapon. Jesus is victorious, but the enemy is still alive and working in the world today.

1. Why doesn't Jesus just wipe Satan out? What does 2 Peter 3:9 say about why Jesus is waiting?

_____

_____

_____

_____

2. God uses the gospel of peace to bring people to repentance—to restore His relationship with people. Read 2 Corinthians 5:17-19. Who is given the job of sharing the gospel of peace with others?

_____

_____

_____

3. In response to what Jesus has done for us, we are to walk in
    faith, confident in whom we have placed our faith. How do
    the following verses describe the life of a Christian soldier?

Ephesians 4:1-2

_____

_____

_____

_____

Philippians 1:27-28

_____

_____

_____

_____

1 Timothy 6:11-14

_____

_____

_____

_____

1 Peter 3:15

_____

_____

_____

_____

apply

In order to share with others the gospel of peace—the reason for your faith—and fend off Satan's attacks, you need to *know* what you believe. A faith based on the truth of God's Word will protect and equip you for the battle against Satan, the father of lies. Your faith can be a lifeline to those who are perishing, pointing them to Jesus, the One who can save them.

1. Read John 3:17 and 1 Peter 3:18. What was Jesus' purpose in defeating Satan? What does this mean for your life today?

   _____

   _____

   _____

   _____

2. Read Acts 2:22-24. What secured Jesus' victory over the enemy? How does this affect your response to temptation and sin?

   _____

   _____

   _____

   _____

3. Read Romans 6:1-8. How did Jesus' victory over sin and death affect His followers? How does this affect the way you see yourself and others?

   _____

   _____

   _____

   _____

4. Read Ephesians 5:1-2,8-10. How are Jesus' followers able to live as a result of what He has done for them? What would your relationships with others look like if you always lived this way?

_____

_____

_____

5. Read Philippians 1:27-28. What does it mean to take a stand for Jesus against the enemy? How would an attitude of confidence and godly character impact your ability to share Jesus with your peers?

_____

_____

_____

_____

reflect

1. What do you appreciate most about what Christ did for you? Why?

_____

_____

_____

2. How has your faith in Christ grown as you have learned more about Him?

_____

_____

_____

_____

3. What are some of the fiery arrows the enemy uses to at-
    tack your shield of faith?

    ....

    ....

    ....

    ....

4. What can you do to strengthen your shield of faith in or-
    der to defend yourself and take a stand for Christ?

    ....

    ....

    ....

    ....

5. Who do you know in your life who needs the gospel of
    peace?

    ....

    ....

    ....

    ....

6. Write a statement of faith, describing what you believe
    about Christ.

    ....

    ....

    ....

    ....

As you conclude this session, consider how your statement lines up with what the Bible says about faith in Christ. Choose one or two Scriptures from this session that you feel you need to keep close to your heart, and then spend some time in prayer asking God to wrap His shield of faith around you. Commit at least one of the Scriptures you chose to memory and share it with a friend.

meditation

Faith comes from hearing the message, and the message
is heard through the word of Christ.

ROMANS 10:17

Note
1. Adapted from Tom Boal, "Knight Without Armor," *The Big Book of Bible Skits* (Ventura, CA: Gospel Light, 1977), pp. 371-373. Used by permission.

cover your head and swing your sword

The law of the Lord is perfect, reviving the soul. The statutes of the Lord are trustworthy, making wise the simple.

PSALM 19:7

Set during the Portuguese colonial period in South America, the movie *The Mission* depicts the Christian conversion of a Portuguese slave trader named Rodrigo Mendoza (played by Robert DeNiro). In one of the most gripping scenes, Mendoza is seen dragging a net full of burdensome weapons and armor up huge cliffs and dangerous waterfalls. Exhausted and covered in mud, he falls at the feet of men from the Guarani tribe—a group of natives he formerly chased, captured and sold off into slavery.

One of the Guaranis grabs a knife and dashes to a bruised Mendoza. He appears ready to quickly execute his enemy. Then, surprisingly, he grabs the rope attaching Mendoza's burden to his chest and cuts him free. Overwhelmed with the grace of forgiveness, the former slave trader bursts into tears as the priests and Guaranis laugh and rejoice in this remarkable act of freedom. Mendoza's weapons are thrown off the cliff, and he enters a whole new realm of freedom in Christ. However, he also enters into a new spiritual arena of battle, as the Portuguese government begins to shut down the church's missions. Mendoza is now a soldier in God's army.

History is filled with many amazing stories of people who exchanged swords of steel for the sword of the Spirit. A steel sword can pierce the heart, yet only the sword of the Spirit can break it. Because we are protected by God's helmet of salvation, we can learn to face spiritual battles with freedom, confidence and hope in Christ.

One of the tricks Satan will use to discourage you as a youth worker is to keep reminding you about past sins, mistakes and character flaws. Just like that filthy net of old weapons and battle armor Mendoza dragged behind him, Satan will use guilt and shame to drag you down by reminding you of sins that have already been forgiven. This is when you need to remember that, in Christ, you have been freed of your former life. As Paul states, you have "put on the new self, which is being renewed in knowledge in the image of its Creator" (Colossians 3:10).

When the good-for-nothing baggage of your former sins has been cut off and rolled straight off a cliff, it is gone, and you are now completely free to love and enjoy an intimate relationship with God. The Holy Spirit gives you the secure hope of your salvation, and the sword of the Spirit enables you to plant the seeds of God's Word into young lives. Once former enemies of God, you are now His child and have been given *His* purpose-filled mission.

The helmet of salvation reminds us that we belong to Jesus
and that we are assured of final victory in battle.
C. PETER WAGNER

cover your head and swing your sword

starter

TRUST ISSUES: Rate the following items as to how reliable they are. Assign a number from 1 to 5 for each one, with 1 being totally untrustworthy and 5 being never-let-you-down trustworthy. After rating each item, answer the questions that follow.

_____ Tacos from a catering truck
_____ A promise from your best friend
_____ Your little brother or sister
_____ Grandma's cookies
_____ Last summer's bathing suit
_____ Relationship advice from Facebook friends whom you haven't met

Note: You can download this group study guide in 8¹/₂" x 11" format at **www.gospellight.com/uncommon/winning_spiritual_battles.zip.**

_____ Your mom's car

_____ The Internet service at the coffee shop

_____ The price of gasoline

_____ A garden gnome (just kidding!)

_____ The messages in TV commercials

_____ The bus schedule

1. What makes something trustworthy?

2. What is the relationship between trust and hope?

3. What is the relationship between trust and truth?

message

The last two pieces of spiritual equipment that Paul urges his readers to pick up are "the helmet of salvation and the sword of the

Spirit, which is the word of God" (Ephesians 6:17). Like the other items that Paul has listed, these are critical items that will enable followers of Christ to stand strong against the enemy's attacks.

the helmet of salvation

Trust, hope and truth are interrelated. In order to trust in something, we first need to be sure that what it claims to be is true. Having this confidence will then help us to place our hope in its continued trustworthiness. The same is true of salvation. Once we are certain that what God claims in His Word is true—that Jesus came "to seek and to save what was lost" (Luke 19:10)—we are able to trust in His promises and place our hope and trust in Him. When we do this, we equip the helmet of salvation.

1. Why is it important for a person in battle to protect his or her head? What are the risks of not wearing protective headgear?

   _____

   _____

   _____

   _____

2. Read 1 Thessalonians 5:8. What other words are used to describe the helmet?

   _____

   _____

   _____

   _____

3. The helmet, or hope of salvation, transforms us also and prepares us to stand for Christ against the enemy. Read

Romans 15:13. How does this verse describe the impact that the hope of salvation can have in our lives?

_____

_____

_____

_____

4. Hope in Christ can secure our victory against Satan. What do these verses say about the source of the power in which we have placed our hope?

Luke 10:19-20

_____

_____

_____

_____

2 Corinthians 3:4-5

_____

_____

_____

_____

the sword of the Spirit

Once we have the belt, breastplate, shoes, shield and helmet in place, we are ready to take up the sword. Notice that Paul lists this item last. The sword is not something a soldier took up lightly—he had to learn to use it and train with it so he could wield it effectively in battle. In the same way, we must learn to use the sword of the Spirit, which is our primary offensive weapon, to be effective in spiritual battle.

The sword of the Spirit is immediately paired with the idea of *praying in the Spirit*. In Ephesians 6:17-18, Paul commands us to *take up* the Word of God as as the sword of the Spirit and to *pray* in the Spirit.

The word "word" in Ephesians 6:17 is *rhema* in the original Greek and refers to the spoken word—an idea that has been said aloud for everyone to hear. The Word of God is not just a religious book with blank ink and white pages, but a living and loud revelation of God Himself.

When we pray in the Spirit, we allow God to lead us to pray His will. The Holy Spirit will guide our prayers as we yield to God's will. By doing this, we are effectively "covering" ourselves with a strong piece of spiritual armor. Note that praying in the Spirit is not about us getting our way, but about us working alongside God, speaking His Word by the power of His Spirit. In this way, the armor of God both starts and ends with our reliance on Him. We begin by recognizing that we must be strong in the Lord (see Ephesians 6:10) and end by praying His truth by the power of His Spirit (see Ephesians 6:17-18).

1. Read John 1:1-2,14. Who is the Word?

    _____

    _____

    _____

    _____

2. Read Psalm 119:9-11. What is the Word?

    _____

    _____

    _____

    _____

3. Read Hebrews 4:12-13. What does the sword of the Spirit do?

_____

_____

_____

4. According to 2 Corinthians 10:3-5, in what kinds of battles do we use the sword to fight?

_____

_____

_____

_____

dig

C. S. Lewis wrote, "Hope is one of the Theological virtues. This means that a continual looking forward to the eternal world is not (as some modern people think) a form of escapism or wishful thinking, but one of the things a Christian is meant to do. It does not mean that we are to leave the present world as it is. If you read history you will find that the Christians who did most for the present world were just those who thought most of the next."[1] Our hope is based on our salvation through Christ, and this hope gives us the ability to live our lives in the way that God intended for us to live them.

1. Read 1 Thessalonians 5:8. What character quality does the helmet of salvation help us to have? How does this quality help us to resist the enemy's attacks?

_____

_____

_____

2. According to Hebrews 10:23, why can we place our trust in the salvation that is available to us through Christ?

_____

_____

_____

_____

3. In military terms, "morale" (also known as *esprit de corps*) refers to a unit's overall hope and belief that it will be able to achieve its stated objectives. Why is it important for soldiers to have good morale? What is the benefit of having hope when facing the enemy?

_____

_____

_____

_____

4. In 2 Timothy 2:15, Paul writes, "Do your best to present yourself to God as one approved, a workman who does not need to be ashamed and who correctly handles the word of truth." What does this mean in terms of how we should handle God's Word?

_____

_____

_____

_____

5. Read 2 Corinthians 10:3-5. What does using the truth of God's Word to demolish strongholds (areas of sin in our

lives), arguments and pretentions (ideas that are contrary to God's Word) allow us to do?

_____

_____

_____

_____

_____

apply

1. How does the hope that you have in Christ help you to mentally and spiritually face challenges from the enemy?

    _____

    _____

    _____

2. What opportunities do you have to study and apply what you are learning from God's Word?

    _____

    _____

    _____

3. What "strongholds," "arguments" and "pretentions" do you face? In other words, in what ways has the enemy been trying to work his way into your mind?

    _____

    _____

    _____

4. How can knowledge and understanding of God's Word protect you from being pulled away from God?

_____

_____

_____

_____

_____

5. How does knowing God personally through the salvation and truth of His Word that He provides help you to better trust Him?

_____

_____

_____

_____

6. In Philippians 4:13, Paul writes, "I can do everything through him who gives me strength." Hope and trust pave the way to victory. Who is the source of power for your I-can-do-it attitude? In what ways are you tapping into that power?

_____

_____

_____

_____

_____

reflect

The story is told of a famous family of trapeze performers who one day decided to train the youngest daughter to "fly." The father coached his daughter up to the high trapeze at the top of the training tent, where she stood many feet above the tent floor. Below her was a safety net, but she was not harnessed to any type of safety cable. The father allowed the young daughter to stand there for a few minutes before he instructed the trapeze to be released. At this point, the daughter turned to him and said, "Daddy, I am afraid, please let me come down." Her father's loving reply was, "Trust me, I know how you feel. Just throw your heart toward the bar, and your body will follow."

1. In Proverbs 3:5-6, we have a similar coaxing from our heavenly Father. What do these verses tell us to do?

    _____

    _____

    _____

    _____

2. What is the result of trusting in God?

    _____

    _____

    _____

    _____

3. In Romans 5:3-5, Paul tells us that the ultimate result of trusting God when we are suffering and facing challenges is hope. What encouragement do you find in these words to face hardship with an attitude of hope and trust?

    _____

    _____

    _____

    _____

4. What level of trust do you see in your relationship with Jesus?

_____

_____

_____

_____

5. What is one area in your life where you find it hard to trust God? What is one step you can take to trust Him to love and care for you (see Hebrews 10:23)?

_____

_____

_____

_____

6. How well do you know God's Word? How can you use God's Word to help you know if an idea, attitude or behavior in your life is godly or based on a lie?

_____

_____

_____

_____

7. Who do you know who can walk with you as you learn to trust God and depend on Him? How can that person assist you?

_____

_____

_____

_____

8. In what ways do you need God to provide you with victory as you stand firmly against the enemy?

_____

_____

_____

_____

Pray about any changes you need Jesus' help to make in order to stand confidently in the face of the enemy's attacks. Also consider how you can support others as you stand strong together. Then, open His Word and learn about His great love and power.

meditation

Let us hold unswervingly to the hope we profess,

for he who promised is faithful.

HEBREWS 10:23

Note

1. C. S. Lewis, *Mere Christianity* (New York: Harper Collins, 2001), p. 134.

contact the Commander-in-chief frequently

Listen to my cry for help, my King and my God, for to you I pray.
In the morning, O Lord, you hear my voice; in the morning I lay my
requests before you and wait in expectation.

PSALM 5:2-3

There are five seconds to go in the game, and your team is down by three points. The center inbounds the ball to the guard, who dribbles up the court. Three seconds to go. The guard makes a little head fake and slips free of the defender. One second to go. He lets the ball go from half court as the buzzer goes off. Swish!

This isn't a shot made all that often. These high lobs into the air typically fall way short, or go long into the stands, or just smack against the backboard with a reverberating thud. In life, there will be times when your prayer life seems to be doing the same. You toss those half-court prayer shots and hope they go in. The results? Lots of air balls. Inconsistencies. Misses. No points. Frustration.

Prayer is simply our way to know and communicate with God. Yet all too often, we dismiss the importance of prayer until a really big-ticket item comes along and we think, *Oh boy, I'd better pray about this one!* So we lob up a half-court prayer shot, turn around, walk away and usually forget whether or not God answered the prayer.

In strictly basketball terms, not too many games are won at half-court. In strictly military terms, not many battles are won without constant communication between the commander and soldier. So why would prayer be any different?

We are to pray *consistently* and *constantly*. We are to pray believing that God will hear and answer our prayers. We are to pray to know and worship God. We are to be expectant when we pray and listen for God's voice to whisper to our soul. We are to pray to know God. To follow Him. To love Him. To serve Him. To abide in Him.

C. S. Lewis once said, "I don't pray to change me. I pray because prayer changes me." Prayer will equip you to fight the tests, temptations and trials you face each day. Prayer will change you, and it will change the lives of the students to whom you minister.

So seek God fervently in prayer today. By maintaining constant communication with your heavenly Father, you'll never have to throw a desperate prayer shot at the buzzer.

I have been driven many times to my knees by the overwhelming
conviction that I had nowhere else to go. My own wisdom, and that
of all about me, seemed insufficient for the day.
ABRAHAM LINCOLN

contact the Commander-in-chief frequently

starter

GOOD COMMUNICATION: Have the group members form pairs. Give each pair a piece of paper, a pencil and a book or magazine to use as a writing surface. The members will sit back to back on the floor, and then one person will lead the other as they both try to draw the same simple picture (house, flower, kite, snowman). The pairs cannot look at each other's papers or name what they are drawing (for example, they can't say, "I'm drawing a house"). The one leading can only give verbal descriptions for the location

Note: You can download this group study guide in 8$\frac{1}{2}$" x 11" format at **www.gospellight.com/uncommon/winning_spiritual_battles.zip.**

of the sketch on the paper (top, bottom, left side), the direction to draw (left, right, up, down) and the kind of line/shape to draw (diagonal, curve, length or size of line/shape). After about 10 minutes, have the members of each pair compare pictures. Discuss the following questions:

- Did your pictures look the same?
- What made this activity difficult to do?
- Which was easier: being the leader or the follower? Why?
- What communication skills would make this activity easier to do well?
- How would this activity be different if you were paired up with God?

message

Now that we are in full gear with the belt of truth, the breastplate of righteousness, the shoes of the gospel of peace, the shield of faith, the helmet of salvation and the sword of the Spirit, we are ready for action. However, to be effective in the battle, we still need one more important thing: direction from our Commander. This is where prayer comes in. Prayer is our connection to God, our leader in battle against the enemy. This is why, after listing all of the pieces of spiritual armor, Paul writes in Ephesians 6:18:

And pray in the Spirit on all occasions with all kinds of prayers and requests. With this in mind, be alert and always keep on praying for all the saints.

1. The words "and pray" indicate that prayer is an integral part of putting on the armor of God and taking a stand

against Satan. According to this verse, how are we supposed to pray?

_____

_____

_____

_____

2. When are we to pray (see also 1 Thessalonians 5:16-18)?

_____

_____

_____

_____

3. What kinds of prayers should we give to God?

_____

_____

_____

_____

4. What attitude should we have when we pray?

_____

_____

_____

_____

5. Read James 1:2-8 and Philippians 4:4-9. What do these verses say about how we should pray?

_____

_____

_____

_____

6. Read Romans 12:12 and Colossians 4:2-3. How do these verses describe the mindset that promotes good communication with God?

_____

_____

_____

_____

_____

7. In Ephesians 6:18, Paul says that we are to pray "in the Spirit." What do the following verses tell you about the Spirit's role in prayer?

Romans 8:26-27

_____

_____

_____

_____

Ephesians 2:18

_____

_____

_____

_____

Ephesians 2:22

_____

_____

_____

_____

dig

There are many examples of people in the Bible communicating with the Master and Commander for many different reasons. Some of these include: (1) to express *adoration* (praise and worship) to God; (2) to *confess* (repent of) sins; (3) to ask God to meet their own needs (*petition*); (4) to *intercede* for the needs of others; and (5) to *listen* to God and ask for His instruction. Look up each of the following passages, and then draw a line to the type of prayer it represents.

1 Samuel 3:9	Intercession
Acts 16:25	Confession
Nehemiah 1:11	Thanksgiving
John 17:20-23	Petition
Psalm 51:1	Listening

1. How do these types of prayers enable you to stand strong and resist the enemy?

    _____

    _____

    _____

    _____

2. In 1 Thessalonians 5:17, Paul tells us to "pray continually." What do you think this means?

    _____

    _____

    _____

    _____

3. What does it *not* mean to pray continually?

_____

_____

_____

_____

4. Read Philippians 4:9. What are the benefits of constant communication with God?

_____

_____

_____

_____

5. Read 1 John 5:13-15. Under what conditions can we pray with confidence?

_____

_____

_____

_____

6. Read Romans 8:26-27. What happens when we don't know how to pray?

_____

_____

_____

_____

apply

Learning to pray is a process that takes practice. Just as it takes time to really get to know another person, the more time we spend interacting with God, the better we will know and understand Him. Being intentional about building a strong prayer life will allow God to transform our relationship with Him and empower us to change our world for His sake. Our lives can become one great prayer!

In Philippians 4:4-7, Paul gives us a helpful model for bringing prayer into every area of our lives. As you review each step, write a short prayer and then consider ways that you could incorporate that aspect of prayer into your everyday life. Be creative!

step 1: Praise God and rejoice

"Rejoice in the Lord always. I will say it again: Rejoice!" (Philippians 4:4). Praise straightens out our priorities, helps us remember who God is, and helps us to realize and acknowledge all that He has done for us.

1. Complete this prayer: "Dear God, I praise You for being..."

---

2. What are some ways you can incorporate rejoicing in the Lord into your everyday life?

---

step 2: Repent humbly and honestly
"Let your gentleness be evident to all. The Lord is near. Do not be anxious about anything" (Philippians 4:5-6). Sin creates distance in our relationship with God. Asking God to forgive our sins restores our relationship with Him and brings peace to our lives. We can once again be close to the Lord, "without blemish and free from accusation" (Colossians 1:22).

1. Complete this prayer: "Dear God, please forgive me for . . ."

_____

_____

_____

_____

_____

2. In Psalm 139:23, David writes, "Search me, O God, and know my heart; test me and know my anxious thoughts." How can you make this practice a part of your daily routine?

_____

_____

_____

_____

step 3: Appreciate God for what He has done
"But in everything, by prayer and petition, with thanksgiving" (Philippians 4:6). Thanking God for what He has already done helps us to pray according to His will. When our focus is on recognizing His perfect love and care for us, our prayers will line up with what God wants to do in our lives.

1. Complete this prayer: "Dear God, I thank You for . . ."

---

2. How can you make sure that you are thanking God for all that He has done on a daily basis?

---

step four: You ask and believe

"Present your requests to God" (Philippians 4:6). Offering prayers for specific needs helps us to see what God is doing. If we write down specific requests, we can track how God chooses to answer us, and we change how we pray if we see a clear direction that God is taking.

1. Complete this prayer: "Dear God, today I ask that You . . ."

---

2. What is one way that you can record and track your prayer
    requests?

    ....

    ....

    ....

    ....

step five: Expect to hear God's voice

"And the peace of God, which transcends all understanding"
(Philippians 4:7). Knowing that God is near and listening to us—
even when we are waiting to hear a specific answer from Him—can
be a great source of peace and comfort. Prayer is a relationship,
not a vending machine, and a strong relationship is characterized
by listening to each other.

1. Complete this prayer: "Dear God, I am listening, and this is
    what I hear . . ." (write down any thoughts, impressions,
    verses or reminders that come into your head as you listen).

    ....

    ....

    ....

2. Why is it sometimes difficult to listen to God? What can
    you do to relax during your prayer time and just listen for
    God's voice?

    ....

    ....

    ....

    ....

step six: Receive it and write it down

"Will guard your hearts and your minds in Christ Jesus" (Philippians 4:7). Some answers to prayer will be quite obvious, while others will be subtler. The better we know God's Word, the easier it will be for us to discern if God is speaking to us in a specific way. As Paul writes in 1 Thessalonians 5:21, "Test everything."

1. Complete this prayer: "Dear God, I hear You saying . . ."

    _____

    _____

    _____

    _____

2. How will you continue to build your skill in knowing God through His Word?

    _____

    _____

    _____

    _____

Note that each step in this model for prayer from Philippians 4:4-7 begins with a word that spells "PRAYER": Praise, Repent, Appreciate, You ask, Expect and Receive.

reflect

1. What are two ways in which you have seen the benefits of prayer in your life or in the life of someone you know?

    _____

    _____

    _____

2. Reflect on the PRAYER model in the apply section. Which of the steps are you most comfortable in doing?

_____

_____

_____

_____

_____

3. Which steps are you least comfortable with doing, or tend to overlook?

_____

_____

_____

_____

_____

4. How would investing in your prayer conversations with God affect your life? The lives of those for whom you pray?

_____

_____

_____

_____

_____

5. How would it help you handle the challenges that the enemy brings?

_____

_____

_____

_____

_____

6. What is one thing you would talk to God about if you
   could see Him standing in front of you?

7. What, if anything, keeps you from asking Him every day
   in prayer to meet your needs and/or for His help?

8. Have you ever heard God speak to you? Explain.

9. How did you know it was His voice?

10. Joshua 1:9 says, "Be strong and courageous. Do not be terrified; do not be discouraged, for the Lord your God will be with you wherever you go." God promises to give us strength when we are weak, answers when we are confused, courage when we are afraid, and hope when we feel defeated. What is one issue or concern about which you feel you need some answers or encouragement?

_____

_____

_____

_____

_____

Take some time in prayer asking God for what you need, believing that He will faithfully answer you at the right time.

meditation

If any of you lacks wisdom, he should ask God, who gives generously to all without finding fault, and it will be given to him. But when he asks, he must believe and not doubt.

JAMES 1:5-6

HOME HW WORD

WHERE PARENTS GET REAL ANSWERS

Get Equipped with HomeWord...

LISTEN
HomeWord Radio
programs reach over 800 communities nationwide with *HomeWord with Jim Burns* – a daily ½ hour interview feature, *HomeWord Snapshots* – a daily 1 minute family drama, and *HomeWord this Week* – a ½ hour weekend edition of the daily program, and our one-hour program.

CLICK
HomeWord.com
provides advice and resources to millions of visitors each year. A truly interactive website, HomeWord.com provides access to parent newsletter, Q&As, online broadcasts, tip sheets, our online store and more.

READ
HomeWord Resources
parent newsletters, equip families and Churches worldwide with practical Q&As, online broadcasts, tip sheets, our online store and more. Many of these resources are also packaged digitally to meet the needs of today's busy parents.

ATTEND
HomeWord Events
Understanding Your Teenager, Building Healthy Morals & Values, Generation 2 Generation and Refreshing Your Marriage are held in over 100 communities nationwide each year. HomeWord events educate and encourage parents while providing answers to life's most pressing parenting and family questions.

A Ministry with *Jim Burns*

In response to the overwhelming needs of parents and families, Jim Burns founded HomeWord in 1985. HomeWord, a Christian organization, equips and encourages parents, families, and churches worldwide.

Find Out More
Sign up for our FREE daily
e-devotional and parent e-newsletter
at HomeWord.com, or call 800.397.9725.

HomeWord.com

Small Group Curriculum Kits

Confident Parenting Kit

This is a must-have resource for today's family! Let Jim Burns help you to tackle overcrowded lives, negative family patterns, while creating a grace-filled home and raising kids who love God and themselves.

Kit contains:
- 6 sessions on DVD featuring Dr. Jim Burns
- CD with reproducible small group leader's guide and participant guides
- poster, bulletin insert, and more

Creating an Intimate Marriage Kit

Dr. Jim Burns wants every couple to experience a marriage filled with A.W.E.: affection, warmth, and encouragement. He shows husbands and wives how to make their marriage a priority as they discover ways to repair the past, communicate and resolve conflict, refresh their marriage spiritually, and more!

Kit contains:
- 6 sessions on DVD featuring Dr. Jim Burns
- CD with reproducible small group leader's guide and participant guides
- poster, bulletin insert, and more

Parenting Teenagers for Positive Results

This popular resource is designed for small groups and Sunday schools. The DVD features real family situations played out in humorous family vignettes followed by words of wisdom by youth and family expert, Jim Burns, Ph.D.

Kit contains:
- 6 sessions on DVD featuring Dr. Jim Burns
- CD with reproducible small group leader's guide and participant guides
- poster, bulletin insert, and more

Teaching Your Children Healthy Sexuality Kit

Trusted family authority Dr. Jim Burns outlines a simple and practical guide for parents on how to develop in their children a healthy perspective regarding their bodies and sexuality. Promotes godly values about sex and relationships.

Kit contains:
- 6 sessions on DVD featuring Dr. Jim Burns
- CD with reproducible small group leader's guide and participant guides
- poster, bulletin insert, and more

Tons of helpful resources for youth workers, parents and youth. Visit our online store at www.HomeWord.com or call us at 800-397-9725

HOME WORD
WHERE PARENTS GET REAL ANSWERS

Parent and Family Resources from HomeWord
for you and your kids...

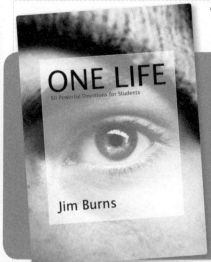

One Life Kit

Your kids only have one life – help them discover the greatest adventure life has to offer! 50 fresh devotional readings that cover many of the major issues of life and faith your kids are wrestling with such as sex, family relationships, trusting God, worry, fatigue and daily surrender. And it's perfect for you and your kids to do together!

Addicted to God Kit

Is your kids' time absorbed by MySpace, text messaging and hanging out at the mall? This devotional will challenge them to adopt thankfulness, make the most of their days and never settle for mediocrity! Fifty days in the Scripture is bound to change your kids' lives forever.

Devotions on the Run Kit

These devotionals are short, simple, and spiritual. They will encourage you to take action in your walk with God. Each study stays in your heart throughout the day, providing direction and clarity when it is most needed.

90 Days Through the New Testament Kit

Downloadable devotional. Author Jim Burns put together a Bible study devotional program for himself to follow, one that would take him through the New Testament in three months. His simple plan was so powerful that he was called to share it with others. A top seller!

Tons of helpful resources for youth workers, parents and youth. Visit our online store at www.HomeWord.com or call us at 800-397-9725

Small Group Curriculum Kits

Confirming Your Faith Kit

Rite-of-Passage curriculum empowers youth to make wise decisions...to choose Christ. Help them take ownership of their faith! Lead them to do this by experiencing a vital Christian lifestyle.

Kit contains:
- 13 engaging lessons
- Ideas for retreats and special Celebration
- Solid foundational Bible concepts
- 1 leaders guide and 6 student journals (booklets)

10 Building Blocks Kit

Learn to live, laugh, love, and play together as a family. When you learn the 10 essential principles for creating a happy, close-knit household, you'll discover a family that shines with love for God and one another! Use this curriculum to help equip families in your church.

Kit contains:
- 10 sessions on DVD featuring Dr. Jim Burns
- CD with reproducible small group leader's guide and participant guides
- poster and bulletin insert
- 10 Building Blocks book

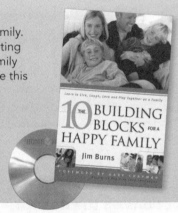

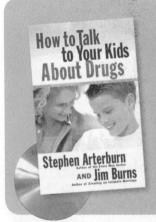

How to Talk to Your Kids About Drugs Kit

Dr. Jim Burns speaks to parents about the important topic of talking to their kids about drugs. You'll find everything you need to help parents learn and implement a plan for drug-proofing their kids.

Kit contains:
- 2 session DVD featuring family expert Dr. Jim Burns
- CD with reproducible small group leader's guide and participant guides
- poster, bulletin insert, and more
- How to Talk to Your Kids About Drugs book

Tons of helpful resources for youth workers, parents and youth. Visit our online store at www.HomeWord.com or call us at 800-397-9725

HOME WORD
WHERE PARENTS GET REAL ANSWERS